Transactional Analysis
for Social Workers
and Counsellors

Library of Social Work

General Editor:
Noel Timms
Professor of Social Work Studies
University of Newcastle upon Tyne

Transactional Analysis for Social Workers and Counsellors

An Introduction

Elizabeth Pitman

Routledge & Kegan Paul
London, Boston, Melbourne and Henley

For Peter

First published in 1984
by Routledge & Kegan Paul plc

39 Store Street, London WC1E 7DD, England

9 Park Street, Boston, Mass. 02108, USA

464 St Kilda Road, Melbourne,
Victoria 3004, Australia and

Broadway House, Newtown Road,
Henley-on-Thames, Oxon RG9 1EN, England

Printed in Great Britain
by Redwood Burn Limited
Trowbridge, Wiltshire

Library of Congress Cataloging in Publication Data

Pitman, Elizabeth, 1940–
Transactional analysis for social workers and counsellors.
(Library of social work)
Bibliography: p.
Includes index.
1. Transactional analysis. 2. Social service.
3. Counseling. I. Title. II. Series.
RC489.T7P57 1983 616.89'145 83–11118

ISBN 0–7100–9581–3 (pbk)

Contents

Preface

The impetus for writing this book stems primarily from
several years' experience in teaching transactional
analysis. I have taught the merely curious, people who
want to use transactional analysis to help them resolve
problems, and social workers and counsellors who see it
as a potentially useful and effective tool for social
work practice. However, much of the available literature
on transactional analysis can prove an obstacle to people
who are interested in the subject, despite the wish of
Eric Berne, its originator, to present the ideas in ways
that made them accessible to almost everyone. (References
to writers other than Berne have been put in both the text
and the index. Since Berne's ideas are to be found
throughout his writings, a comprehensive list of his
publications is given in the references but details do
not normally appear in the text.)

Sometimes, the presentation of the theory is so over-
simplified, over-enthusiastic and unrealistic in the claims
made for the efficacy of transactional analysis that it
reinforces, for the sceptic, a view that this is yet
another fashionable but lightweight theory. Alternatively,
the theoretical ideas can be lost in a sea of complex
jargon, making it difficult for a newcomer to the subject
to gain a clear understanding of the basic concepts.

Transactional analysis, like other personality theories,
has a semi-technical language of its own compounded, in
this case, by several other problems. Confusion can
sometimes arise because words in common use are used with
very specialised meanings, e.g. Parent, Adult, Child and
games. Sometimes, the language used reflects the consumer
society in which transactional analysis has its roots,
e.g. trading stamps, plastic strokes. These words may
have little, if any, meaning in less consumer-oriented
societies. Finally, some words reinforce the view that

transactional analysis is a superficial, rather than credible approach to problem-solving, e.g. warm fuzzies, pig parent. In this book, I hope to bridge this gap between the over-simple and the complex by writing a clear and credible introduction to transactional analysis theory and use. This book is intended for social workers and counsellors who are unfamiliar with, but interested in transactional analysis. It does not purport to be a training manual, but for those people who are interested in developing further knowledge of the theory and practice of transactional analysis, further information is given in Appendix 1. The emphasis throughout has been on the presentation of transactional analysis as a useful approach to social work and counselling practice, and I have been at pains to present the theory as a framework for people to use in understanding problems and working out ways of resolving them, rather than as a creed for living (Kovel, 1978).

Being an introduction, this book does not attempt to provide a complete coverage of every aspect of trans-actional analysis theory and practice, nor to examine all the contradictions within the literature. The intention has been to introduce the main theoretical concepts, with an emphasis on those I have found most pertinent to social work and counselling practice, as well as to provide some ideas about the ways in which the theory can be used.

In attempting to keep jargon to a minimum, and in the interests of clarity, I have sometimes modified terminology but, in each case, have indicated the conventional terminology, so that readers can make the connection between this and other books on transactional analysis.

I take full responsibility for the choices I have made in presenting transactional analysis theory in this book.

Throughout the text, I have used words such as 'flexible', 'constructive', or 'appropriate' when referring to emotional and behavioural problems. Whilst the meanings of these words are specific, there are rarely any absolute rights or wrongs about what constitutes, for example, 'appropriate' behaviour in any one situation. What is right or appropriate for one person might be totally inappropriate for another, yet both views about behaviour might be valid. Hence, a deliberate vagueness in defining 'appropriateness', etc., too closely is deliberate as it enables readers to apply their own criteria, attitudes, values and judgments.

I have used the convention of referring to a social worker or counsellor as 'she' and to other people as 'he',

unless referring to specific cases. Fictitious names have
been used throughout in order to preserve confidentiality.
The words 'social worker' and 'counsellor', and 'social
work' and 'counselling' are used interchangeably, in
order to avoid too much repetition.

   The glossary at the end of the book gives brief
definitions of the transactional analysis terms used in
the text.

Acknowledgments

My thanks and acknowledgments go to the many students, social workers and counsellors whose interest in transactional analysis has encouraged me to write this book. Particular thanks are due to the people who have given generously of their time in contributing to the case material in Chapter 9. My thanks also go to those people with whom I have, in a variety of ways, been able to use transactional analysis as a mode of working. I am grateful to Professor Noel Timms, Dr Ron Walton and Miss Barbara Butler for their encouragement and constructive reading of my text, to Philippa Brewster (RKP) for her help and support, and to Mrs Cynthia Diggins for her patient typing of early drafts. I also acknowledge, with thanks, the permission given by Faber & Faber and Harcourt Brace Jovanovitch to use an extract from T.S. Eliot's poem *The Love Song of J. Alfred Prufrock*.

Finally, my gratitude and thanks go to Peter Pitman for his constructive help, support and encouragement throughout the writing of this book.

Any shortcomings that remain in the text are entirely my responsibility.

Chapter 1

An introduction to transactional analysis

Transactional analysis provides an explanation of
personality development and structure, communication,
behaviour and relationships between people. It is based
on the humanistic belief that there exists within
individuals an impetus for emotional growth and the
development of autonomy. Knowledge and use of transactional analysis can help people to come to a better
understanding of themselves and others and to make
attitude and behavioural changes which can result in
happier, more fulfilled and constructive lives.

Transactional analysis was originally developed by
Eric Berne (1910-1970), an American psychiatrist with a
Freudian training. His theoretical ideas grew out of
his clinical observations of patients, whilst his
philosophy stemmed from his disagreements with much
traditional psychoanalytic practice. He was opposed to
a paternalistic or medical model of therapy, in which
workers tended to take on the major responsibility for
analysing clients' problems and deciding on solutions,
whilst clients remained passive and uninvolved in working
on their difficulties. Instead, he argued that people
could take an active part in, and be responsible for,
understanding their problems and working out ways of
solving them. Berne believed that his first responsibility
was to help people get better, rather than to deal with
the origins of problems. This meant moving away from a
model in which change occurred after exploration, analysis
and insight had been considered, to one in which rapid
and effective change in current emotions and behaviour
was the prime aim. More detailed exploration and analysis
occurred only if this proved to be a prerequisite for
change.

Although transactional analysis was originally developed
as a group therapy, it is now used with individuals, couples
and families (Dusay and Steiner in Kaplan and Sadcock, 1972;
Gellert and Wilson, 1978; Lester, 1980; O'Connor, 1977;
Tweed, 1980). Its use has been extended well beyond the
psychiatric setting in which Berne worked. Transactional
analysis is used within a range of statutory and voluntary
settings, residential establishments, including penal ones,
education, industry and management (Adams, 1974; Byron, 1976;
Jesness et al., 1972; Reynolds, 1979; Roth, 1977). It is
used for a variety of client problems, ranging from work with
the mentally ill, the physically ill and handicapped, the
elderly, and children and adolescents with a range of problems
(Arnold and Simpson, 1975; Baum-Baicher, 1979; Clayton and
Dunbar, 1977; Garber et al., 1976; Hale et al., 1974; Schiff
and Day, 1970).

Transactional analysis can be used for clarifying and
assessing situations (Wilson, 1979), as an intervention
strategy and as a tool for monitoring and evaluating change.
It is most effective when the concepts are shared with
clients as it provides a structure which enables them to make
better sense of their internal and external worlds, as well
as providing ideas about problem solving and behavioural
change. The overall goal of transactional analysis is to
help people develop and achieve autonomy. Individual
practice is based on a clear contract between client and
counsellor in which the specific goals of intervention are
clearly specified. Transactional analysis, whilst it rests
on a few basic ground rules, is rich in variety, styles and
orientations. It is often used with other techniques, e.g.
gestalt therapy, behavioural therapy, psycho-drama, and
guided fantasy. It can also enrich other approaches to
social work practice and behavioural change, e.g. task-
centred and psycho-social casework, marital and family
therapy. The strategies embodied within transactional
analysis are used both within and outside interviews, thus
enhancing and accelerating the process of problem solving.

TRANSACTIONAL ANALYSIS IN OUTLINE

Although the various aspects of transactional analysis
theory are treated separately and in greater detail in
subsequent chapters, a general survey is provided at this
point so that, as each separate piece of theory is
presented, it can be fitted into the overall framework.

The aspect of theory dealing with personality structure,

function and development is called structural analysis.
Transactional analysis (a term which is used both for the
total theory and for the aspect of theory dealing with
communication) explains communication patterns, whilst
games analysis explores the ulterior or double-level
communication that is used in some relationships. Script
analysis looks at the way in which reactions to early
experiences continue to influence later behaviour.

Transactional analysis uses familiar, everyday words
to describe the unique interaction of external stimuli
with the internal world and the resultant affective and
behavioural responses. |The thoughts, feelings and
behaviours which make up an individual's personality are
conceived as falling into three distinct patterns. Berne
called these patterns ego states.| An ego state is defined
as a 'system of feelings which motivates a related set of
behaviour patterns' (Berne, 1966). Berne named the three
basic, or primary, ego states Parent, Adult and Child,
and classified them in terms of their differing behavioural
characteristics. When referring to ego states, rather
than to people, the words Parent, Adult and Child are
written with initial capital letters. In order to avoid
too much repetition, these words will sometimes be used
alone, e.g. Parent, rather than Parent ego state. When
behaviour is described in terms of the ego state involved,
the ego state is said to be 'used', 'activated' or
'cathected'. Alternatively, a person's behaviour is said
to be 'in' a particular ego state or 'coming from' a
particular ego state. Ego states are represented graphically
by three discrete circles arranged vertically and normally
in descending order of Parent (P), Adult (A) and Child (C)
(see Figure 1.1).

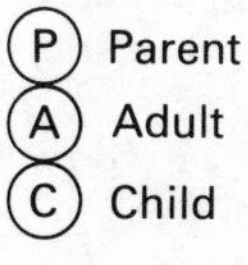

P Parent
A Adult
C Child

FIGURE 1.1 Primary ego states

Behaviour coming from the Parent ego state is characterized by nurturing or being critical and judgmental, and is
influenced by the values and attitudes a person holds.
Behaviour coming from the Adult ego state is characterized
by thinking about things, collecting data and making
choices and decisions. Behaviour coming from the Child

ego state is characterized by emotional responses to situations, e.g. feeling happy, sad, joyful or angry, or behaving in impulsive, creative, curious or inquisitive ways.

The personality of a new-born baby consists solely of a Child ego state, in which primitive, uncensored needs, feelings and instinctual urges predominate. The Adult ego state begins to emerge when a small child starts making connections between cause and effect, asking questions and making decisions. The Parent ego state begins to emerge when a small child incorporates values and opinions from both parents and others, and begins to look after himself and others. The three ego states emerge during early childhood and are usually developed by adolescence, although all three can continue to change throughout a person's lifetime.

Strokes, or units of recognition, and messages about how to think, feel and act provide the stimuli through which small children experience the world. These normally come primarily from parents or parent-substitutes. The kind of stroking pattern experienced, and messages received, by a baby, together with his reactions to them result in an early childhood decision about his life position or attitude towards himself and others. These early messages and the subsequent decisions and life position taken by a child become, in time, his life plan or script. Subsequent behaviour is then based on responding to situations in ways which reinforce the early decisions, life position and script and make the world a safe and predictable place for the individual concerned.

Although personality development takes place within a physical and emotional environment, Berne also suggested that there is an existential dimension to life, with each individual having to decide how to structure his time between birth and death. Early experiences and decisions provide the rationale for each person's pattern of time structuring, whilst the content involves communication, or transactions, either between people or between internal ego states. Communication is described and analysed in terms of vectors, or communication paths, going from one or more ego states in an initiator, to one or more ego states in a respondent, or between two ego states within an individual. A stimulus and its response constitutes a transaction (see Figure 1.2).

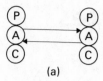

(a)

a transaction between
two people
FIGURE 1.2

(b)

internal transaction
between ego states

Transactions may be simple or complex, and in either
case they may be clear and unambiguous or confusing and
contradictory. The latter type often serve to reinforce
unhelpful behaviour and early decisions.

A person's behaviour, communication and pattern of
time structuring all occur within the context of his
frame of reference, or his perception, based on early
experiences, decisions and life plan, of himself, others
and the world in which he lives. Whilst a person's frame
of reference may be flexible and constructive, enabling
him to lead a fulfilled and generally happy life, some
early experiences and subsequent decisions can be
destructive and unhelpful, resulting in a life which may
be problematic in a variety of ways.

The practice of transactional analysis, which is based
on clear and explicit contracts between workers and
clients, can accelerate change in a variety of situations
and problems, including those resistant to other, more
traditional forms of intervention. It can provide a
framework enabling unhappy people to replace early
unhelpful decisions with new and more constructive ones,
and for working out and practising changes which can
result in happier, more fulfilled and autonomous lives
for the people concerned. It can also be used by people
who are relatively problem-free to enhance personal
understanding and interpersonal relationships.

The overall goal of transactional analysis, helping
people achieve autonomy, requires the development or
redevelopment of the capacities for awareness, spontaneity
and intimacy, characteristics which are viewed as the
components of autonomy. The underlying philosophical
assumption of transactional analysis is that people can
change destructive and unhelpful feelings, attitudes and
behaviour in favour of autonomy.

Chapter 2

The theory of ego states

Berne developed ideas about personality structure and
behaviour from his clinical observations. He suggested
that the various behaviours exhibited by people arose
from three different components he called ego states.
He classified these ego states on the basis of their
external behavioural manifestations and on three basic
assumptions about human behaviour. Firstly, everyone
retains memories of their early childhood experiences
and the feelings and reactions attached to them. In
later life, these can often be reactivated inappropriately,
thus interfering with and skewing realistic appraisals of
current situations. Secondly, everyone (unless severely
brain damaged) is capable of developing the ability to
think rationally, to make decisions and to mediate between
the demands of the internal and external worlds. Thirdly,
everyone experiences, as a child, some form of parenting,
either in his own family, foster home or children's home.
From these parenting experiences, people learn behaviours
which enable them to look after themselves and others,
although not necessarily in a constructive manner.

The Child ego state is characterized by emotional
responses to situations, reflecting the way in which small
children, with only a limited ability to think and
conceptualize, respond to the world around them. The
Adult ego state is characterized by thinking and rational
behaviour, finding out about things, processing information
and making decisions. The Parent ego state is characterized
by taught concepts, relating to values, attitudes and
opinions as well as knowledge about how to look after
oneself and others.

The classification and description of these primary ego
states is called first order analysis. (In order to avoid

too much repetition, the three primary ego states, Parent, Adult and Child will usually be referred to without the prefix 'primary' unless this is necessary for clarity of presentation.) Within each of these primary ego states, various subdivisions have been postulated, and the classification and description of these is called second order analysis. The subdivisions are of two kinds. One represents the content or structural aspect of each ego state as it develops between birth and adulthood. (In order to produce a consistent framework, I am departing from the forms normally used in the literature and using instead a framework in which the secondary ego states of the Child are referred to as C_c, A_c and P_c, the secondary ego states of the Adult as C_a, A_a and P_a and the secondary ego states of the Parent as C_p, A_p and P_p.) The other represents the behavioural or functional aspect of each ego state (Joines, 1976; Porter, 1975).

THE CHILD EGO STATE - FIRST ORDER ANALYSIS

When a baby is born, his behaviour and responses to situations stem from his Child ego state, as neither the Adult nor Parent ego state is yet developed. From the moment of birth, interaction occurs between a baby's unique self, consisting of physiological and physical factors, and his environment. For example, in some families a child may be well cared for, both physically and emotionally, and this is reflected in loving handling and care. In others, he may be well cared for physically, but his emotional needs ignored or neglected. Some families may smother a child emotionally, thus discouraging his emotional growth and exploration of the outside world, whilst in other families a child may be physically and emotionally abused and neglected. Cultural norms also influence the environment in which a child grows up. These relate to such things as prescribed behaviour about handling, male and female roles and so on. It is from this interaction between the external world and the child's physical, physiological and emotional constitution that each person's unique personality emerges.

Because a small baby has extremely limited cognitive and thinking ability, his reactions to his needs and experiences are mainly emotional or affective. As a child grows up and develops other aspects of his personality, the Child ego state remains the one in which emotional, affective responses to situations occur. It is also the ego state in which creativity, spontaneity and other childlike but important aspects of the personality are found.

THE CHILD EGO STATE - SECOND ORDER ANALYSIS

Structural characteristics

A more detailed analysis of the primary Child ego state indicates that it contains secondary Parent, Adult and Child ego states within it. The Child within the primary Child ego state (C_c) is all that exists when babies are born. It contains physiological factors, innate needs and primitive, uncensored feelings. From a very early age, the totally egocentric, narcissistic behaviour of small babies is being acted upon and modified by other people, primarily parents. As a result, the early spontaneous feelings that small babies have in response to these external events also remain a part of their C_c ego states.

Small children, before they can think logically, seem to develop a creative and intuitive mode of thinking, which enables them to arrive at accurate and perceptive conclusions without apparently having sufficient data on which to operate. This creative, intuitive thinking is carried out by the Adult within the Child ego state (A_c).

The world of small children is bounded by grown-ups who tell them what they ought to do, and who reward or reprimand them according to their responses to parental demands. Children are not always given rational explanations for the often seemingly confusing and contradictory rules and behaviours that adults impose on them. The behaviours that children learn in response to adult expectations become, in time, internalized and automatic, occurring even when parents no longer demand them. Cleaning one's teeth, washing one's neck, being polite, sharing with others, are all examples of early learned behaviour. Alongside these behavioural responses, children may also have affective reactions to the demands made on them, such as feelings of bewilderment, anger, fear or sadness. These learned behaviours and affective reactions, which act as inhibitors on the uncensored, primitive, spontaneous needs and responses of C_c are carried out by the Parent in the Child ego state (P_c).

Thus, the primary Child ego state, whilst it consists mainly of emotional responses to the demands of the outside world, also contains all the innate feelings with which children are born, intuitive thinking and creativity, as well as early, learned behaviour, many of which become automatic responses to situations (see Figure 2.1).

Child
{ behavioural adaptations to and feelings about the demands of the external world
— intuitive thinking and creativity
{ primitive, uncensored feelings, needs and responses

} Child: thinking, feeling and behaving characterized by emotional responses to situations

FIGURE 2.1   Primary Child ego state with structural characteristics

The following provides an example of behaviour stemming from various parts of the Child ego state. A small child, happily scribbling on the wallpaper, is behaving from C_c, i.e. spontaneously and without regard for the demands of the outside world. When he is smacked for being naughty, he may react with anger or sadness from P_c. When left alone again, he might be tempted to continue the C_c behaviour by scribbling on some books, but decides, using A_c, that although nothing has been said about books, he might be smacked again, which would result in further sad and angry feelings. Thus A_c intuitive thinking, together with P_c feelings, act together to inhibit the spontaneous and impulsive behaviour of C_c.

Functional characteristics

Functional analysis is concerned with the way in which individuals use their ego states, both internally and in their relationships with others. From a functional point of view, the Child ego state is divided into two parts, known as the Free Child (sometimes known as the Natural Child) and the Adapted Child. Both of these functional ego states have a helpful and unhelpful aspect (see Figure 2.2) (Woollams and Brown, 1979).
(The convention in the literature is to use the words 'positive' and 'negative', but this can give rise to confusion, as the words are rarely used in their correct grammatical sense. I have therefore replaced these with 'helpful' and 'unhelpful' in relation to the functional

aspects of the Child and Parent ego states and to the
discussion of strokes in Chapter 4.)

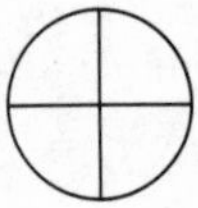

Helpful Adapted Child   Helpful Free Child

Unhelpful Adapted Child   Unhelpful Free Child

FIGURE 2.2   Child ego state - functional

The Helpful Free Child in both children and adults,
expresses itself in spontaneous, creative, fun-loving
and autonomous ways. Behaviour is first processed
through the Adult, enabling it to be realistic and
constructive, and enhancing creativity, autonomy, personal
fulfilment and relationships with others. Unhelpful
Free Child behaviour is not processed through the Adult
and this can result in impulsive, destructive behaviour,
in which the needs for personal safety are ignored, e.g.
through the abuse of drugs, alcohol or cigarettes, and
in which the individual acts without regard for the
consequences of his behaviour or the realistic demands of
the outside world. People who have had inconsistent
parenting in which the limits set on their behaviour when
they were children were arbitary, contradictory or
destructive often use their Free Child inappropriately,
being unable to set constructive limits on their own
behaviour in later life. Thus, inappropriate use of Free
Child behaviour can result in problems, both for the
person expressing the behaviour and others with whom he
comes into contact.

Helpful Adapted Child behaviours provide constructive
adaptations to the demands of the outside world and act
as useful limitations on the potentially destructive
aspects of the Unhelpful Free Child. These behaviours
can also be processed through the Adult ego state, but
they often become automatic, requiring little Adult
processing. Greeting rituals, saying 'please' and 'thank
you', personal hygiene and table manners are all examples
of Helpful Adapted Child behaviour.

All parents pass on to their children precepts about
what feelings and behaviours are acceptable within the
family. Sometimes, parental precepts are destructive or
over-restrictive but a small child, powerless to compare

these with other views of the world, has to learn acceptable affective and behavioural responses to them. Whilst these learned responses may be realistic at the time, they can, in later life, act as archaic, restrictive and unhelpful parts of the personality. These feelings and behaviours stem from the Unhelpful Adapted Child, and are rarely processed through the Adult, but remain linked with archaic feelings from the past, rather than being viewed in the light of current information about situations. It is important to recognise that children may sometimes respond to situations in ways which stem from misinterpretations of, or misperceptions about, parental precepts and demands. For example, one child who is told to 'work hard and succeed' may grow up to do so, enjoying success in work, leisure, and personal relationships, whilst another child, given the same parental message, might become a 'workoholic', unable to succeed in any area of his life other than work, and being unhappy and unfulfilled in personal relationships and in his leisure time activities.

Three styles of Unhelpful Adapted Child behaviour have been identified (Holloway in Barnes, ed., 1977). Two result from the child learning to manipulate the world around him, although complying with parental expectations, whilst the third stems from aggressive or rebellious behaviour as a response to parental demands. Children who are over-protected and whose growth to independence is discouraged, learn to please others by being unable to do things for themselves and by being confused and helpless. In later life, such individuals seek out relationships which reinforce their helplessness and confusion. This style of behaviour comes from the Helpless Adapted Child. Children who learn to conform rigidly to parental expectations become compliant, responding to others' needs and demands, whilst ignoring their own. As adults, such individuals are over-helpful to others, compliant and conforming, spending much of their time looking after others, whether or not it is needed. This style of behaviour comes from the Over-helpful Adapted Child. (The word 'over-helpful' replaces Holloway's word 'helpful' in order to avoid confusion with my use of the word 'helpful' in categorizing the various aspects of the functional Adapted Child. It is also a more accurate description of the behaviour under discussion.) Some children learn that they can only get attention by being aggressive, or find that rebellious, aggressive behaviour is encouraged by their parents. As adults, such individuals tend to respond automatically with similar behaviour,

whether or not it is appropriate. This automatic behaviour
stems from the Rebellious Adapted Child.

An example of Unhelpful Adapted Child behaviour is
provided by Mrs Adams, a disabled woman in her sixties,
referred to me by her general practitioner, with vague
and unspecific problems of anxiety and depression. In
our early interviews, Mrs Adams kept up a rambling
monologue which ranged, without any obvious connecting
threads, over her past and present life. It was difficult
to find out why Mrs Adams had been referred, or, indeed,
what she hoped for from social work contact, and early
efforts to find a clear focus for intervention were
unsuccessful. However, a key to some of the issues
concerning Mrs Adams seemed to be found when she said
casually that as a small child she had been told, when
her younger sister was born, that she was responsible
for looking after the baby. It soon became clear that
Mrs Adams had internalized this message so firmly that
she had spent much of her life behaving from the Over-
helpful style of her Adapted Child ego state, constantly
looking after other people, whether or not they needed
or requested help. I used a task-centred approach with
Mrs Adams, designed to help her shift her energy from
Adapted to Free Child. Firstly, she agreed to set a
time limit when seeing a neighbour whom she perceived as
being very demanding and who seemed to share a never-
ending succession of problems with Mrs Adams. Secondly,
she agreed to ask her husband to check out theatre
facilities for the disabled, since she had enjoyed the
theatre before developing a hip disability. Although
this approach dealt, at an apparently superficial level,
with only one aspect of the presenting problem, it seemed
successful. As Mrs Adams used less Adapted Child
behaviour with her neighbour and began to enjoy her Free
Child in going to the theatre, she became more relaxed,
and some of the resentment and anger about the demands
of others, which had been forcefully and bitterly
expressed in her earlier interviews with me, disappeared.

THE ADULT EGO STATE - FIRST ORDER ANALYSIS

The first ego state to develop separately from the Child
is the Adult ego state. This ego state begins to
develop at about eighteen months and it is normally fully
functioning by the age of twelve. Definitions of the
Adult are similar to those found in traditional psycho-
dynamic theory. It is regarded as the ego state

characterized by thinking and rational behaviour. It is attuned to current reality, both external and internal, and it acts as a mediator between internal needs and wishes and the demands of the external world. Thus, the Adult is the part of the personality which collects and processes information, examines options, estimates probabilities and makes decisions about how to act. Ideally, Parent and Child behaviours are processed through the Adult, which then acts as the mediator of the personality, deciding when and how it is appropriate to use behaviour from the other ego states.

For example, a counsellor who is tired after a long and exhausting day is asked to see a depressed client who has arrived at her office without an appointment. The counsellor's internal dialogue, within a transactional analysis framework, might be as follows:

Parent: It's my duty to see him, as he's obviously
           very depressed and I really ought to give
           him some of my time.
Adult: I appreciate he needs some time, but I
           really am too tired to be much use to him.
           I'll see him briefly now and offer an early
           appointment tomorrow morning.
Child: I'm tired and I want to go home!

In this example, assuming the counsellor decides on the Adult solution, it can be seen that the Adult has mediated between the Parent 'oughts' and the Child 'wants' and reached a reasonable compromise. Whilst the Adult solution might vary from one occasion to another, the important thing is to consider all aspects of a situation, before arriving at a solution. In this example, the level of the client's distress might have been such that the counsellor would have decided on a longer interview. Had she done so, she would have needed to find an effective way of dealing with her own Child needs by ensuring that, once at home, she relaxed and did something she enjoyed.

THE ADULT EGO STATE - SECOND ORDER ANALYSIS

Structural characteristics

Although Berne's framework for the structure of the Adult was not consistent with his structural analysis of the Child ego state, it is clear from his own descriptions that this would have been appropriate. The structural analysis of the Adult presented here will, therefore, be made in a way that marries Berne's terminology and definitions with the structural framework provided by the Child ego state. Berne's descriptions of the ego states within the Adult refer, firstly, to a childlike quality of charm and openness, coupled with responsible feelings towards others. These characteristics, which Berne subsumed under the term Pathos, I see as being the characteristics of the Child in the Adult (C_a). Secondly, the Adult ego state consists of the ability to process data objectively and this I see as being a characteristic of the Adult in the Adult (A_a). Thirdly, the Adult contains attributes such as courage, sincerity, loyalty and reliability which are part of a universal ethos. These characteristics, which Berne subsumed under the term Ethos, I would see as stemming from the Parent in the Adult (P_a) (see figure 2.3).

Adult   Ethos
        Objective data processing
        Pathos

FIGURE 2.3   Adult ego state - structural

Thinking, information-processing and decision-making by the Adult are all enhanced when it has assimilated ethical and affective behaviours. A person with such an Adult ego state is likely to be emotionally mature, autonomous in behaviour and concerned with societal issues, as well as those of personal happiness and fulfilment (Gillespie, 1976; Goulding, 1974; Krumper, 1977; Kuijt, 1980).

Functional characteristics

When analysed in terms of its function, the Adult ego state is not divided into discrete parts, as are the Child and Parent ego states. Instead it operates as an integrated ego state. Effective use of the Adult enables an individual to decide when and how it is appropriate to use Child and Parent behaviours, arbitrates when there is conflict between the needs of the Child and the demands of the Parent, and protects the Child when it is being threatened by unhelpful Parent attitudes.

There are, however, different views in transactional analysis literature about the way in which the Adult ego

state functions. Some writers argue that it is not, in
fact, an autonomous ego state, but that it is only used
when it is needed to mediate between conflicting Child
and Parent needs. Others suggest that the Adult ego
state is fully autonomous, being able to make and carry
out decisions, even when the Child and/or Parent are in
opposition. My own experience suggests that, for
behaviour to be constructive and appropriate, particularly
when problem solving is concerned, the Adult ego state
can and must be used to make sense of situations, work
out the available options and decide on strategies for
behaviour. Effective use of the Adult can be hindered by
archaic and destructive Child feelings and Parent
attitudes and opinions, as these can act to sabotage
Adult efforts at change. It is usually necessary to
address oneself to all three ego states, working through
Child and Parent blocks to the process of change, and
using the rational strength of the Adult as an ally in
evaluating what needs changing and how this can be
achieved.

THE PARENT EGO STATE - FIRST ORDER ANALYSIS

With the development of the separate Parent ego state
from about the age of six years, a small child has all
three primary ego states available for use. The Parent
ego state in a child is influenced both by the kind of
parenting he receives and the cultural and social environment in which he lives. The role of parent (or parent-
substitute) in relation to young children is a rich and
complex one. It consists of providing physical and
emotional nurturing, the passing on of skills and knowledge, and giving information about the norms, values,
attitudes and behaviours considered acceptable within the
family and society at large. Precepts about attitudes,
values and behaviour are also passed on through the
educational, social and cultural environment in which a
child lives (James and Jongeward, 1973a).

When a child is small, he experiences two main types
of parental influence. Firstly, nurturing which is
designed to meet his physical and emotional needs;
secondly, taught concepts about the values, attitudes
and opinions he should hold. The child gradually
incorporates nurturing behaviours into his own Parent,
thus developing the ability to look after himself and
others, although if the parenting has been destructive,
inconsistent or over-restrictive, the Child's Parent ego

state may incorporate unhelpful parental behaviours (James
and Jongeward, 1975). He also develops an internalized
set of values, attitudes, and prejudices about how he and
others ought to think, feel and behave. Once internalized,
these attitudes and behaviours can be expressed externally
as behaviour towards others, or internally, as an
influence on the Child ego state. When there is an
internal Parental influence, the Child ego state reacts
with feelings to this influence. For example, a child
who is taught that children should be 'seen and not heard'
by rigid, authoritarian parents, might accept this as a
reasonable Parent belief and, in his turn, when an adult,
act in an authoritarian way to his own children. Since
this internalized Parent might also act as a rigid,
repressive influence on the Child, the person may
experience Child feelings of sadness and depression as an
emotional reaction, both to the original exhortations of
his parents, and to the current influence of his own
Parent ego state.

Thus, a person can incorporate behaviours learnt from
others and subsequently behave in a similar fashion from
his own Parent ego state. Alternatively, when the Parent
acts as an influence on the Child, a person usually
responds by doing what is expected of him by the Parent
ego state, even if this results in unhappy feelings or
non-autonomous behaviour.

THE PARENT EGO STATE - SECOND ORDER ANALYSIS

Structural characteristics

When the Parent ego state is examined in terms of its
structure, the influence of parents, siblings, relations
and so on can be seen within the various parts of the
Parent. These also occur within the Child and the Adult,
but as the significance of people outside the family is
much stronger as a child grows up, the developing Parent
ego state is open to a wider variety of influences (see
Figure 2.4).

The parenting behaviours which have been described in
the literature seem, curiously, to concentrate mainly on
the restrictive aspects of parenting and in so doing,
important and necessary aspects of the Parent are under-
valued (Boulton, 1978). The Parent in the Parent (P_P) is
seen as being critical, controlling and judgmental or,
alternatively, being over-protective, inconsistent or

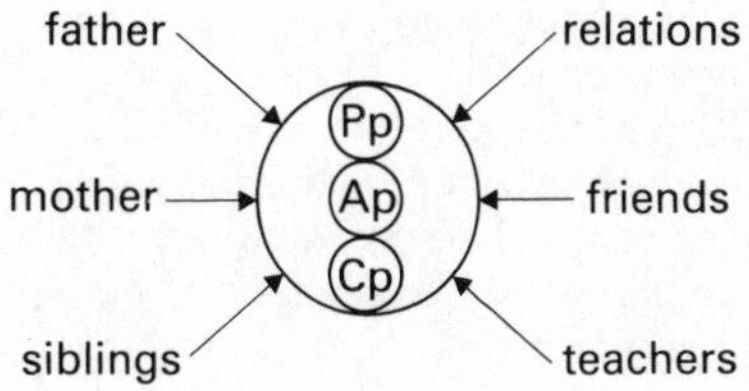

FIGURE 2.4   Parent ego state - structural

ambivalent. The Adult in the Parent (A_p) is seen as
being unfeeling, inflexible, over-organised or emotionally
distant. The Child in the Parent (C_p) is said to be
demonstrated when a person is over-needy and helpless,
seeking others to take care of him.

Functional characteristics

Functionally, the Parent, like the Child, is divided into
two parts, each with a helpful and unhelpful aspect.
These are called Nurturing Parent and Controlling Parent
(sometimes called Critical Parent) (see Figure 2.5).

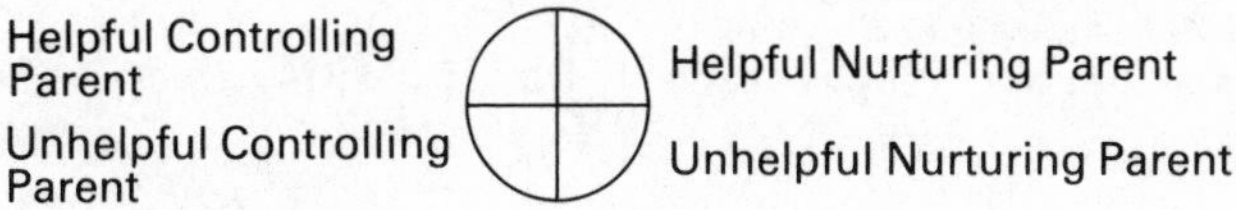

Helpful Controlling
Parent   Helpful Nurturing Parent
Unhelpful Controlling   Unhelpful Nurturing Parent
Parent

FIGURE 2.5   Parent ego state - functional

When a person uses his Helpful Nurturing Parent, either
inwardly as an influence on the Child, or outwardly,
towards others, he is able to give realistic and appropriate nurturing and protection which encourages the development of autonomy in self and others. Unhelpful Nurturing
Parent behaviour may do too much nurturing by doing
things for others, which are not needed, thus encouraging
dependency, or it can be over-permissive, thus failing
to set realistic limits on self and others.

When a person is using Helpful Controlling Parent, he
is able to give constructively critical feedback and to
set realistic behavioural limits on his own and others'

behaviour. This is done from a basis of care and concern, rather than as a punishing action. An Unhelpful Controlling Parent is demonstrated when a person criticizes himself or others in destructive ways. Good social work practice often involves the use of Helpful Nurturing and Controlling Parent ego states. Nurturing Parent behaviour occurs when offering clients support and protection in their struggles to resolve problems. The Controlling Parent is used when giving critical feedback and setting limits as a necessary and constructive part of the process of change.

CHILD DEVELOPMENT - A SUMMARY

When a child is born, his personality consists solely of C_c innate needs, feelings and impulses. From about six months onwards, he begins to appreciate himself as a person separate from his mother and by about eighteen months he has developed his own simple thinking (A_c) in relation to the outside world. From about three years, P_c emerges as the child reacts to parental limits on his behaviour. From about eighteen months onwards, the separate Adult is emerging as the child begins to gain skills and knowledge and to develop his cognitive and thinking abilities. From about six years, the separate Parent ego state emerges, as the child begins to incorporate, as well as react to, parental expectations and behaviour. By the age of twelve, all three primary ego states are normally operational (Levin, 1974) (see Figure 2.6).

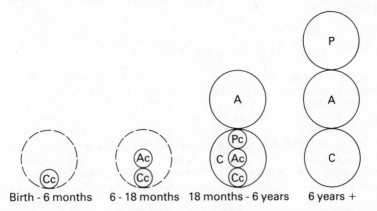

Birth - 6 months   6 - 18 months   18 months - 6 years   6 years +

FIGURE 2.6 Child development of ego states

Other than the innate C_c, all the ego states are
potentially capable of further development. However, in
Western culture, there is considerable emphasis during
childhood on the development of the Adult and Parent,
often at the expense of the creative, intuitive, spontaneous Child (Klein, 1980). When this occurs, energy
is concentrated mainly in the Adult and Parent ego
states. At puberty, the sexual aspects of the Child
become manifest, and energy gradually becomes more evenly
distributed between the ego states. Ideally, adults
should be able to use all their ego states in creative,
flexible and autonomous ways.

ENERGY IN EGO STATES

The concepts relating to energy in ego states are based
on the constancy hypothesis, which suggests that the
amount of psychic energy within an individual remains
constant, although it flows between ego states (Dusay,
1977). The word cathexis is used to represent this flow
of energy. The ego state which is cathected, i.e. into
which energy has flowed, is said to be in the executive.
This is not necessarily the ego state being behaviourally
expressed. For example, in an intermediate treatment
group, a social worker might be using Free Child in having
fun with the group members, but keeping his Adult in the
executive in order to monitor what is going on around
him, and to ensure that no-one is being excluded or
bullied by others. Later, relaxing over a meal, energy
may shift entirely into the Free Child ego state, with
the Adult deciding that this was the appropriate ego
state for the situation. When this occurs, the Adult,
temporarily at least, no longer needs to have executive
responsibilities.

Ideally, energy should be able to move freely and
sometimes rapidly between ego states, so that responses
to situations are appropriate and realistic. Individuals
who are unable to achieve this under-use or over-use one
or more ego states at the expense of others. The way in
which energy is used depends primarily on the experiences
people have had as children and their reactions to these.
For example, a child whose spontaneous, creative Free
Child was unduly restricted whilst his Adult was
encouraged by 'workoholic' parents, may find that he has
too much energy bound up in his own Adult. As a result,
he may be unable to use his Free Child by switching off
from work or study in order to enjoy himself. Conversely,

a child whose thinking abilities were discounted may find it difficult to use energy in his Adult ego state, and may behave in a confused and helpless manner in relation to thinking things through and coming to decisions. Sometimes current experiences and events can result in temporary problems of energy flow. For example, the grief and sadness following bereavement can result in energy, temporarily at least, being frozen into the Child ego state, thus making it difficult for decisions to be made. As the bereaved person gradually comes to terms with his loss, energy normally flows back into the Adult, and it again becomes possible to think clearly and to make decisions.

Energy distribution and use can be visually represented by the use of egograms or ego state portraits (Dusay, 1977) (see Figure 2.7).

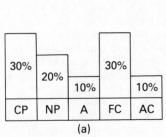

an egogram   ego state portrait
FIGURE 2.7

BOUNDARIES IN EGO STATES

A person who is able to use all his ego states flexibly can switch appropriately between them, is aware of which ego state is cathected, and knows when he is using two or more ego states simultaneously. When this occurs, ego states are seen to be discrete entities, with permeable boundaries through which energy flows freely. There are four kinds of boundary problem with ego states, any one of which can result in varying degrees of destructive behaviour. These are problems of contamination, exclusion, lesions and lax boundaries.

Contamination is probably the commonest boundary

problem, occurring when ego states do not function as
discrete entities. Parent-Adult contamination occurs as
prejudice when Parent opinions and values masquerade as
Adult data. Racial and sexual prejudice, in which
spurious reasons, coming from a contaminated Adult, are
given as a rationale for the prejudice, are a good
example (see Figure 2.8(a)). Adult-Child contamination
occurs when Child fears and anxieties are expressed in
the form of irrational fears, delusions and phobias, and
in which spurious Adult data is given as a rationale for
the fear (see Figure 2.8(b)). There is often a double
contamination, as Parent prejudices are maintained by
scared Child feelings, and vice versa (see Figure 2.8(c)).
Child-Parent contamination expresses itself as confusion,
and usually results from an unsatisfactory attempt to
reconcile conflicting Child needs with Parent precepts
and expectations (see Figure 2.8(d)).

(a)

(b)

(c)

(d)

Parent-Adult contamination	Adult-Child contamination	Parent-Adult + Adult-Child contamination	Parent-Child contamination (note: ego states changed in order in Figure 2.8(d))

FIGURE 2.8

Exclusion occurs when only one or two primary ego
states are used. A person who excludes his Parent ego
state lacks a sense of values and is unable to behave in
a responsible or caring fashion to self or others (see
Figure 2.9(a)). A person with an excluded Adult behaves
in a confused and turbulent way as he is unable to cathect
his Adult in order to mediate between the demands of the
Parent and Child and the external world (see Figure 2.9(b)).
A person with an excluded Child is unable to respond
affectively to situations (see Figure 2.9(c)). When both
Parent and Adult ego states are excluded a person is
infantile, impulsive and chaotic, unable to think things
through with the Adult and unable to control his behaviour
or nurture himself or others (see Figure 2.9(d)). When

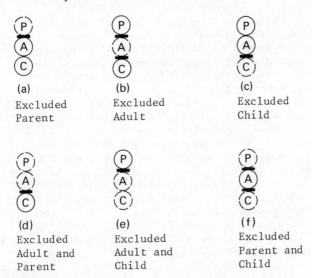

(a)   (b)   (c)

Excluded   Excluded   Excluded
Parent   Adult   Child

(d)   (e)   (f)

Excluded   Excluded   Excluded
Adult and   Adult and   Parent and
Parent   Child   Child

FIGURE 2.9

the Adult and Child ego states are both excluded, a person
is over-nurturing or controlling and unable to respond
emotionally to situations or to think clearly (see Figure
2.9(e)). When the Parent and Child are excluded, a person
is robot-like, unable to respond affectively to situations
or to use his Parent to nurture himself or others or to
set limits on his behaviour (see Figure 2.9(f)).

Lesions occur as 'sore points' within ego states.
When something touches the lesion, there is an over-
reaction in terms of irrational, uncontrollable behaviour.
Whilst lesions can occur in the Parent and Adult, they
occur most frequently in the Child. When someone has
been emotionally or physically injured in childhood by a
traumatic experience or series of experiences, a similar
situation in later life can trigger off memories from
childhood, and lead to apparently irrational behaviour.
For example, a man who was frequently beaten as a child
might hit someone who gives him a friendly, affectionate
thump, interpreting it as an aggressive act (see Figure
2.10(a)).

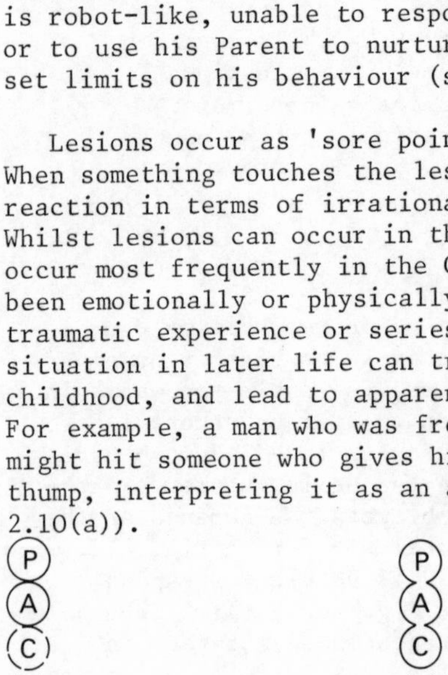

(a)   (b)

Lesions   Lax boundaries

FIGURE 2.10

Lax boundaries occur when energy moves too freely between ego states. There is little Adult control, and behaviour can often 'change with the wind' and be agitated and confused (see Figure 2.10(b)).

THE ADULT PERSONALITY

The focus in this chapter so far has been primarily on the development, content and functioning of ego states in childhood, although the implications for later behaviour and use have also been briefly explored, particularly in relation to problem behaviour. However, as most social workers and counsellors deal with adults as much as, if not more than, children, some comments about the adult personality seem necessary. Clearly individuals vary enormously in personality structure and function: what is seen as fulfilling and autonomous behaviour to one person may seem restrictive to another. Despite this, some general statements can be made about 'normal' behaviour as a basis from which to explore those problems of personality and relationships which are the focus of much social work and counselling practice. When people have problems of an intra- or inter-personal nature, they are usually connected with varying degrees of difficulty in using ego states creatively and flexibly. (I am excluding here problems of a social or economic kind that are beyond the control of the individual.) If people are to develop autonomy in themselves and the ability to make close and loving relationships with others, they need to be able to use all three ego states flexibly and effectively.

The Child is essential as it is the main source of affective, joyful, creative and spontaneous behaviour. When used constructively, it enhances personal well-being and fulfillment and enriches relationships with others. The Adult is essential as it enables individuals to mediate between the internal demands of the Child and Parent, and those of the external world. It is also the part of the personality in which the very necessary process of thinking and decision-making occurs. The Parent is essential as it enables individuals to look after themselves and others, to give constructive feedback when necessary and to set realistic limits on behaviour. People need a Parent ego state to deal with those areas of knowledge and experience where knowledge alone is inadequate. Ethical issues cannot be understood or resolved by purely empirical and factual analysis, but require value-judgments and beliefs, backed up by available information. Social work principles such as client self-determination and unconditional positive regard (Biestek, 1961) are clear examples of Parent values linked to Adult thinking.

Within transactional analysis literature, there has been a tendency to devalue the Parent and Adult and to see the feeling Child as the 'king' (or 'queen') of the ego states. The Adult, in particular, has come to be devalued, with the Pathos and Ethos aspects of an integrated Adult being virtually ignored by many writers. As a result, the Adult has come to be seen as a computer, operating objectively and without feelings. Since feelings are judged to be an essential facet of human personality, this narrow interpretation understandably results in a devaluing of the Adult, with the essential contributions that it can make to the integrated, mature personality being lost or ignored. In the same way, descriptions of the Parent have focused almost entirely on the unhelpful aspects of nurturing and controlling in the Parent ego state, although latterly the constructive aspects of the Parent and the value of using and developing Parent ego state behaviours in therapeutic practice have been acknowledged by several writers.

As a result of these unhelpful interpretations of the Parent and Adult, the Child has, in some instances, come to be over-valued. Whilst problems often stem from under-use of the Child, too great an emphasis on the Child ego state alone can, in my experience, result in people being encouraged to act out archaic and destructive feelings as an end in itself. It is essential to involve the Adult in examining the archaic elements of the Child, to provide more up to date and relevant information and help seek out options for change (Karpman, 1971). The Parent is needed to provide support during the often difficult process of change. An integrated, mature person develops the constructive aspects of all his ego states, in both their structural and functional aspects, as well as the ability to use these ego states flexibly in his relationships with both himself and others.

Under-valuing of the Adult and Parent has occurred, I think, because the concepts relating to the primary ego states have been over-simplified. Berne regarded each ego state as having a thinking, feeling and behavioural component. Subsequently, some writers have come to see the Child as the feeling, affective part of the personality,

the Adult as the thinking part, and the Parent as the
part containing taught concepts and beliefs. A more
accurate, though still clear and simple approach is to
consider the Child as primarily the affective part of
the personality, the Adult as primarily the thinking part
and the Parent as primarily the part containing taught
concepts and beliefs. In this way, the value of each ego
state to the integrated and autonomous personality can be
more easily appreciated, with dysfunctional behaviour being
seen as stemming from under-use, over-use or inappropriate
use of any of the ego states that make up the personality.

Chapter 3

The theory of communication

Although structural analysis has much in common with traditional psychoanalytic theory, transactional analysis, as a theory of communication, is more closely aligned to interactionist and systems frameworks. Communication is analysed in terms of its verbal and non-verbal components and the ego states involved. A single transaction, which takes place along paths or vectors between people or between internal ego states, consists of a stimulus and its response. Transactions are analysed in terms of the ego state involved in a stimulus, that to which the stimulus is directed and the ego state from which a response actually comes and is received by the initiator. As will be seen, responses do not always come from the ego state a sender hoped to activate. Transactions are classified into three main types - complementary, crossed and ulterior.

In the graphical representation of transactions, the initiator is always put on the left, with the stimulus passing from left to right, and the respondent is put on the right, with the response passing from right to left. The examples of transactions given in this chapter are intended merely as brief, illustrative cameos and, as such, they lack a detailed contextual framework and may appear somewhat mechanistic.

COMPLEMENTARY TRANSACTIONS

The following criteria define a complementary transaction:
    (a)   only two ego states are involved;
    (b)   the stimulus and response vectors are parallel;
    (c)   the response comes from the ego state to which
         the stimulus was directed, and passes back to the
         ego state from which the stimulus originated;

(d)   verbal and non-verbal aspects of the communication
      are congruent;
(e)   communication can take place between any of the
      ego states (first or second order) in each person
      involved in the transaction.

The following examples illustrate some of the complementary transactions that can occur in social work and
counselling settings. In an intermediate treatment
setting, the communication between workers and children
who are enjoying canoeing, swimming or walking, would
consist of Child - Child transactions; in a residential
setting, a social worker comforting an unhappy child
would use Parent - Child transactions; in a social skills
group, a client expressing Child anxiety about his ability
to learn new social behaviour might be seeking Adult
feedback; in a counselling interview a client involved in
an Adult discussion about handling debts might be seeking
Parent support and approval for his plans for dealing
with them.

Figure 3.1 gives a brief example of the way in which
complementary transactions are presented graphically in
transactional analysis. A social worker and his team
leader are discussing a request for short-term care.

Social worker: level tone of voice and concerned
                 expression.
Stimulus: 'Mrs X is very depressed about having
                 to care for her mother, but she
                 doesn't want her to go into a home.
                 I think the situation will deteriorate
                 unless we can offer temporary care, so
                 that Mr and Mrs X can have a holiday.'
Ego states: Adult - Adult.
Team leader: interested, questioning voice and
                 expression.
Response: 'You seem to have considered this
                 carefully. I'll second your application
                 for temporary care.'
Ego states: Adult - Adult.

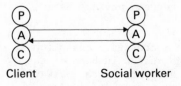

Client   Social worker

FIGURE 3.1 Complementary transaction

CROSSED TRANSACTIONS

The following criteria define a crossed transaction:
   (a)   three or four ego states are involved;
   (b)   the vectors are not normally parallel and often,
         though not always, cross during the transaction;
   (c)   the response does not normally come from the ego
         state to which the stimulus was directed;
   (d)   verbal and non-verbal aspects of the communication
         are congruent;
   (e)   communication can take place between any of the
         ego states (first or second order) in each person
         involved in the transaction.

As crossed transactions are rather more complex than
complementary ones, four different examples are given to
illustrate their variety. Each example deals with a
situation in which a client seeks financial help from a
social worker. The client is requesting financial help
over the weekend because he has lost his giro cheque.

   Client: anxious voice and expression.
   Stimulus: 'I've lost my giro again, so I've
                      come to get some help from you. I
                      can't possibly feed the kids over the
                      weekend otherwise.'
   Ego states: Child stimulus seeking Parent response.
   Social worker: level, questioning tone of voice.
   Response: 'You know we don't have any funds and
                      the DHSS are closed. It does mean
                      managing over the weekend, but I
                      imagine your mother will help you out.'
   Ego states: Adult response, hoping to activate
                      Adult.

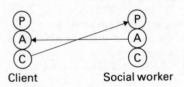

Client   Social worker

FIGURE 3.2   Crossed transaction between primary ego
states

   Figure 3.2 shows a conventional crossed transaction
occurring between the primary ego states in both of the
people concerned. Normally, an analysis of the primary
ego states provides sufficient information for under-

standing interaction. When a breakdown in communication occurs, it can happen because, although a transaction appears to be complementary, it is shown to be a crossed transaction when it is analysed within a second order framework (see Figure 3.3).

Client:	smiling and unconcerned.
Stimulus:	'I've lost my giro again, but I know you'll help me out.'
Ego states:	Free Child stimulus seeking Nurturing Parent response.
Social worker:	critical, angry tone of voice.
Response:	'I'm afraid you're wrong about that - you'll have to manage this time and be more careful in future.'
Ego states:	Controlling Parent to Adapted Child.

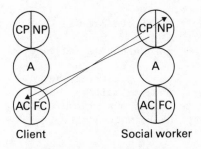

Client   Social worker

FIGURE 3.3 Crossed transaction between secondary (functional) ego states

Sometimes, the vectors are parallel and again, at first sight, the transaction appears to be complementary, but as four ego states are involved, it is a crossed transaction (see Figure 3.4).

Client:	laughing and unconcerned.
Stimulus:	'I've lost my giro *again*! If you can't help me out, I'll probably have to pinch some food.'
Ego states:	Child stimulus, hoping to activate Child response.
Social worker:	level tone of voice.
Response:	'You know we can't help you out, but I'm not sure that stealing is really a good option - would you like to look at alternatives.'
Ego states:	Adult hoping to activate Adult.

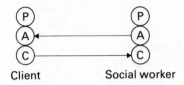

Client   Social worker

FIGURE 3.4 Crossed transaction with parallel vectors, involving four ego states

Sometimes, only three ego states are involved. This is known as an angular, crossed transaction (see Figure 3.5) (Klein, 1980; Woollams and Brown, 1974).

Client:	looking anxious and upset.
Stimulus:	'I've lost my giro again - but I know you'll help me.'
Ego states:	Child hoping to activate Parent response.
Social worker:	firm, but concerned attitude and tone of voice.
Response:	'I realize you must be worried, but I'm not really able to bail you out this time. Let's discuss alternatives.'
Ego states:	Parent hoping to activate Adult.

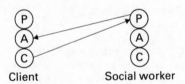

Client   Social worker

FIGURE 3.5 Angular crossed transaction

ULTERIOR TRANSACTIONS

The following criteria define an ulterior transaction:
  (a) three or four ego states are involved;
  (b) there are two levels of message, one verbal (social level) and one non-verbal (psychological level);
  (c) the social and psychological levels of the message are incongruent, and often contradictory;

(d)   communication can take place between any of the
      ego states (first or second order) in each person
      involved in the transaction.

Ulterior transactions are more complex than either
crossed or complementary ones, as they involve indirect
ways of relating to others. The verbal level of the
transaction is socially acceptable, whilst the non-verbal
level is the 'real' message. For instance, someone who
wants to initiate a sexual relationship may tender an
invitation on the lines of the 'come and see my etchings'
theme, rather than making a direct statement about his
sexual intentions. When four ego states are involved, the
transaction is known as an ulterior duplex transaction.
Figure 3.6 gives an example of such a transaction. It
occurs between a single-parent father, who feels he needs
his daughter's help at home, and his daughter, who is
under supervision for failing to attend school, and who
colludes with her father's wish for help from her.

Father: looking depressed and sounding anxious.
Stimulus: 'I don't know how I'll manage when you
               go back to school.'
Ego states: Social level: Adult - Adult information.
               Psychological level: Child - Parent,
               seeking nurturing.
Daughter: looking and sounding concerned.
Response: 'I know I ought to go, but you need me
               here.'
Ego states: Social level: Adult - Adult information.
               Psychological level: Parent - Child
               response.

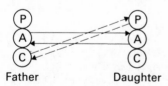

Father   Daughter

FIGURE 3.6 Duplex ulterior transaction

Sometimes, only three ego states are involved, although
there are still both verbal and non-verbal levels. This
type of transaction is known as an ulterior angular one.
It is sometimes referred to as the 'salesman's transaction',
as the sender is aware that, beneath the verbal stimulus,
he is sending out a non-verbal message, designed to

manipulate the Child or Parent in the other person to
behave in a way which meets the sender's wishes. Figure
3.7 gives an example of an ulterior angular transaction.
It occurs between a social worker who is having difficulty
in placing an adolescent in a foster home, and a foster
parent who already has his full 'quota' of foster children.

Social worker: anxious, but cajoling expression and
                 tone.

Stimulus: 'I've got an awful problem at present –
                 a teenager who really needs a good
                 home. It's such a pity you won't
                 consider an extra child – you're just
                 the sort of person he needs.'

Ego states: Social level: Adult – Adult information.
                 Psychological level: Adult – Parent,
                 seeking help.

Foster parent: sounding flattered and looking pleased.

Response: 'We...ell, it would be difficult, but
                 I suppose we could manage.'

Ego states: Social level: Adult – Adult information.
                 Psychological level: Parent – Adult
                 response.

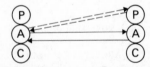

Social worker   Foster parent

FIGURE 3.7   Angular ulterior transaction

One variety of ulterior transaction is known as the
'gallows' transaction. This name is used when people
describe their own destructive behaviour with smiles or
laughs and others respond by laughing with them. By
making light of such behaviour, everyone involved colludes
with and reinforces it.

TRANSACTIONS AND INTERNAL FRAMES OF REFERENCE

Responses sometimes redefine or reinterpret a stimulus
in order to maintain an internal frame of reference.
When this redefinition occurs, the transactions are known
as blocking or tangential ones (Schiff, 1975). Schiff
suggests that, in the course of growing up, a child

develops his own unique frame of reference. This is based
on an individual's ego state development, early decisions,
life position and script. It provides an affective,
cognitive and behavioural 'set' through which an
individual defines himself, others and the environment.
Some individuals, particularly those with unhelpful
scripts and life positions, use a mechanism known as
redefining, in order to reinforce their early decisions
and to make the world a safe and predictable place. This
is an internal mechanism which is used as a defence
against stimuli which seem to be inconsistent with a
person's frame of reference. When this occurs, an
individual is unable to respond flexibly and appropriately
to stimuli, using instead tangential, blocking or other
kinds of ulterior transactions which serve to reinforce
his frame of reference.

In tangential transactions, stimulus and response
either address different issues, or address the same
issue from different perspectives, with the result that
people seem to talk past and not to each other. An ongoing
series of tangential transactions result in the people
involved feeling that the conversation is going round in
circles, with the original issue being lost or ignored.
The following is an example of a tangential transaction,
which occurred in a counselling situation in which I was
seeing Beth and her boyfriend. Beth was a competent,
intelligent young woman, with a demanding job she did
well, a stable relationship with her boyfriend and close
and valued friendships. Despite this, Beth was unhappy
with herself, feeling that she failed to live up to her
expectations of herself and seeing her work and her
personal life in a pessimistic light. In order to
reinforce a frame of reference in which she saw herself
as unsuccessful and inadequate, Beth spent much of her
time redefining situations through the use of tangential
and other types of ulterior transaction. In our interview,
the following dialogue occurred.

Beth's boyfriend: 'When you come home from work, I
                     don't really want to hear too much
                     about your job, as I want us to
                     enjoy our evenings together.'
Beth: 'There, I told you, you're always
                     saying I'm no good at my job.'

Despite the fact that the original comment concerned
a particular facet of their relationship, Beth redefined
it, by going off at a tangent and making it a general
comment about her alleged incompetence at work, thus

using the comment in a distorted way in order to reinforce
her own view of herself as unsuccessful.

Blocking transactions occur when communication is
blocked and deflected by disagreements about definitions
of the issue under discussion. Committee and other
meetings often provide a rich source of such transactions.

INTERNAL TRANSACTIONS

Internal transactions occur when individuals engage in a
dialogue between ego states, in which the demands of the
Parent, the thinking ability of the Adult and the needs
of the Child are all involved.   Figure 3.8 illustrates
an internal dialogue occurring as part of a decision-
making process, in which the Adult has mediated between
the exhortations of the Parent and the feelings of the
Child and reached a reasonable compromise between them.

Parent: 'I ought to write that report now.'
Adult: 'That report must be ready by 5 p.m.'
Child: 'I hate writing reports, especially
                 when I've had a hard week.'
Adult solution
(mediator):   'I'll have a coffee break, then shut
                 myself in my office until I've done,
                 but I'll make sure I relax this
                 evening!'

FIGURE 3.8 Adult acting as executive, mediating between
Child and Parent

DIAGNOSING EGO STATES

Ego states can be identified by analysing the transactions
that occur between people and the influence that one
person's style of transacting might have on another
person (behavioural and social diagnosis) (Falkowski et al,
1980). They can also be identified by a person's reported
experience of the internal dialogue between ego states,

TABLE 1 Behavioural clues to ego state diagnosis

	Nurturing Parent	Controlling Parent	Adult	Free Child	Adapted Child
Words	I love you I like you good splendid	should ought must always	how why what interesting	want now won't I feel	can't wish I wonder try
Voice	tender comforting loving concerned	condescending righteous critical judgmental	even precise calm questioning	loud energetic happy enthusiastic	whining placating angry worried
Gestures, posture, expression	smiling physical touch e.g. hug	frowning pointed finger upright	thoughtful open alert	spontaneous relaxed uninhibited	sad depressed hopeless
Attitude	caring loving giving	judgmental authoritarian moralistic	observant clarifying evaluating	curious impulsive creative	compliant pleading demanding

Adapted from Woollams and Brown, 1979.

and by the way in which present feelings in situations
might be linked with past experiences, or past feelings
re-experienced in current situations (historical and
phenomenological diagnosis) (James, ed., 1977).

Behavioural diagnosis is made by analysing words used,
tone of voice, gestures, expression, posture and attitude.
Table 1 gives examples of the kind of clues that enable
a behavioural diagnosis to be made. It is important to
recognise that these give general guidelines rather than
rigid rules, and that as many clues as possible must be
considered in coming to a decision about which ego
states are being used. For example, someone with a
frown, a critical attitude and tone of voice who is using
the words 'ought' and 'should' is far more likely to be
in his Parent than someone using the same words, but
speaking with a level tone of voice and looking calm.
In the latter instance, the words are being used thought-
fully and reflectively from the Adult ego state.

Social diagnosis is made by analysing the interactions
between people in terms of the ego states involved, and
the influence that the ego states used by one person in
the transaction is liable to have on the other person.
For example, someone who uses a consistent Helpless
Child ego state will tend to elicit either Nurturing or
Controlling Parent responses in others.

Historical diagnosis links present feelings and
behaviours to past experiences. Someone who behaves as
his parents did before him is likely to be using Parent
behaviour, whereas if he is feeling and behaving as he
did when, as a small child, he reacted to parental
demands and expectations, he is more likely to be in his
Child ego state.

Phenomenological diagnosis occurs when someone re-
experiences early childhood feelings when faced with a
similar experience. For example, a child who was
encouraged to enjoy physical activities and games may
re-experience early feelings of elation and excitement
as he takes on and succeeds in new physical challenges.

Diagnosis can thus be made from an individual's
reported and subjective feelings, as well as from his
behaviour and the effect he has on others. If two or
more methods of diagnosis lead to the same conclusion,
their validity is strengthened. For example, in a
therapeutic group setting, Carol behaved in a consistent

Adapted Child manner, constantly seeking attention using
words such as 'can't', 'wish', 'try' and looking and
sounding unhappy and confused (behavioural diagnosis).
The group members initially attempted to respond from
Adult and Nurturing Parent, but as Carol was unable to
use any other ego state other than Adapted Child, group
members became critical and over-protective, using
Unhelpful Controlling or Nurturing Parent (social
diagnosis). Carol had always had an unhappy relationship
with her parents. An only child, she felt unwanted and
unloved, and said that she was always being criticized
by her parents and that her attempts, both as a child and
now as an adult, to please them, were always doomed to
failure. Even though Carol had married and was holding
down a responsible job, she was still obsessed with the
need to please her parents and to achieve success in
their terms. She still saw herself as a small, worthless
and helpless child in her parents' eyes and it was clear,
whatever the reality of her parents' attitudes and
behaviour, that Carol had incorporated strong, Unhelpful
Controlling Parent and over-compliant, passive Adapted
Child ego states. Thus Carol, as an adult, continually
tried to please both her own Controlling Parent and her
actual parents and in the process, she often relived
childhood feelings of sadness and frustration as she
failed to satisfy either her Parent or her parents
(historical diagnosis).

THE RULES OF COMMUNICATION

Berne acknowledged that there is the potential for an
infinite variety and richness in human communication, but
he believed that, in general, people use a very narrow
range of transactions, which serve to limit flexibility
and richness in communication. He proposed three 'rules'
which reinforce this rather pessimistic view of human
interaction. These are that with complementary transactions, communication can continue indefinitely,
constituting a necessary, though not the only condition
for a constructive relationship; with crossed transactions,
communication breaks down, resulting in relationships in
which such transactions predominate being unhappy and
unfulfilled; and with ulterior transactions, the
behavioural outcome is determined at the non-verbal rather
than the verbal level. Although Berne does not, in his
discussion about these rules, comment on the kind of
relationship likely to occur when ulterior transactions
predominate, his work on games clearly indicates that

ulterior transactions are liable to result in dysfunctional
and dishonest communication between people.

The use of the word 'rules' in relation to communication
implies a rigidity that seems to be open to question.
For example, whilst communication normally remains open
with complementary transactions, people who use their ego
states in an inflexible and limited way are liable to
employ a narrow range of complementary transactional
stimuli and response patterns which reinforce non-
autonomous relationships and which inhibit emotional
growth and intimacy. Alternatively, people may use
complementary transactions of a destructive nature in
order to reinforce an unhappy relationship using, for
example, mostly Controlling Parent and Adapted Child in
their communication with each other. When complementary
transactions are used in a narrow or destructive manner,
they cannot be said to be the basis of a constructive
relationship between people.

Although people who enjoy a rewarding relationship with
each other normally use a flexible range of complementary
transactions, there will be occasions when the people
involved in such relationships use crossed transactions
within the framework of a basically constructive relationship. For example there are, at times, value and needs
conflicts between people and discussion about these can
result in crossed transactions. If the people concerned
regard disagreement and conflict in a constructive way,
using it as an opportunity for clarifying issues and
working out acceptable compromises, the crossed transactions
occurring as part of the conflict will be short-lived and
lead to problem resolution rather than breakdown. Also,
in a relationship in which ego states are used flexibly,
there will be numerous shifts between ego states as topics
of conversation change. These may result in temporary
crossed transactions, but these should merely signify a
change of direction, rather than breakdown in communication
or an unhappy relationship.

When one person attempts to involve another in an
ulterior transaction, the respondent does not necessarily
have to respond to the non-verbal level. He can genuinely
respond to the verbal level, and ignore the non-verbal
level of the message, he can bring the contradictions
between the two levels into the open or he can bring the
non-verbal level into the open and respond to it in a
non-ulterior manner. Whatever his choice, he can avoid
getting caught up in dysfunctional, ulterior communications.

OPTIONS IN TRANSACTIONAL ANALYSIS

An understanding of interaction and communication in a
transactional analysis framework can be useful in enabling
people to use a variety of options and choices in their
communications with others. A respondent can, as has
already been suggested, choose how to deal with an
ulterior stimulus. Sometimes, people may deliberately
cross a transactional stimulus in order to change the way
in which a conversation is proceeding. This procedure
can be particularly useful when the stimulus is intended
to activate Unhelpful Adapted Child, Nurturing or
Controlling Parent. For example, with a team leader who
consistently uses an authoritarian Controlling Parent
ego state in the hope of activating compliant Adapted
Child in his team, staff can choose a range of responses
if they want to avoid using Adapted Child behaviour.
Three possible choices are given below.

Stimulus:	'Where's that report on the X family? I should have had it yesterday at the latest.'
Ego states:	Controlling Parent hoping to activate Adapted Child.
Response 1:	'It was ready yesterday, but I wanted to discuss it with you before submitting it and you were not available.'
Ego states:	Adult hoping to activate Adult.
Response 2:	'I am sorry. I was off sick yesterday and I've only just finished it.'
Ego states:	Child hoping to activate Nurturing rather than Controlling Parent.
Response 3:	'Oh, come on, don't fuss - an extra day won't make any difference. You'll get an ulcer if you keep worrying about things - come on, let's go out for lunch and I'll buy you a drink.'
Ego states:	Free Child hoping to activate Free Child.

People who have had happy and constructive experiences
in childhood normally develop a flexible, open frame of
reference, which enables them to use a wide range of
transactional stimuli and responses, either to establish
or sustain relationships, or to prevent themselves getting
caught up in ulterior transactions and games. Conversely,
people who have had unhappy childhoods, and who have
negative attitudes towards themselves and others, may
develop an inflexible, closed frame of reference. When
this occurs, they use a limited range of stimuli and

responses in their transactions. This reinforces their unhappy view of themselves and others and prevents the development of open, autonomous relationships. Clearly, communication between two people is more likely to be mutually satisfying if both use their ego states flexibly.

However, it is possible for one person to use a flexible range of transactions, in which all his ego states are used, even when this is not reciprocated by the other person involved in the dialogue. It is also possible to increase flexibility in communication, if the person who has a wide range of transactional responses available uses all three ego states simultaneously in communicating with someone whose normal range of responses is narrow and stereotyped (Karpman, 1971). For example, with Beth I would use a series of verbal and non-verbal transactions, involving my three ego states, in order to help her move from scared, depressed Adapted Child to her Adult and Parent. My Parent attitude would be one of concern, giving Beth permission to reject the unhelpful parts of her Child and Parent ego states; my Adult would give her feedback about the way in which she reinforced her negative view of herself whilst my Child liking for her would reinforce the Parent and Child permissions and encourage her to enjoy herself more. This process gradually enabled Beth to use more of her energy in her Adult, Nurturing Parent and Free Child, rather than being locked into Adapted Child and Controlling Parent.

Conversely, a person who uses all his ego states flexibly might, on occasions, direct a message from one ego state only to all three ego states in another person, with the intention of extending the range of responses in someone whose normal range was limited. For example, with Beth I would give Adult feedback to challenge her Controlling Parent ('do you want to go on believing archaic messages so that you can continue to sabotage your efforts to change?'); suggest ways in which she could use her Adult to reinforce her efforts at change (listing successes rather than failures each week, getting feedback from her boyfriend and others about their view of her); and finally encourage her Free Child to have some more fun (helping Beth to find ways of enjoying herself, e.g. in dancing, relaxing with her boyfriend, seeing friends). This kind of transaction, in which I used my Adult to help Beth think more clearly about what she was doing to herself, about how she would meet Free Child needs and how she would rid herself of archaic Parent messages, gradually enabled her to change

attitudes, feelings and behaviour from destructive to
constructive ones.

Thus, flexibility in using ego states in communication,
a predominance of complementary transactions and an
ability to avoid ulterior transactions are the hallmarks
of good communication and one of the components in the
forming and maintaining of rich and fulfilled relationships between people.

Chapter 4

Stimulus, recognition and structure hunger

STIMULUS AND RECOGNITION HUNGER

Although the main thrust of early transactional analysis
theory was in examining people's behaviour and interaction
in the 'here and now', the incompleteness of this framework for understanding personality and behaviour resulted
in further developments in theory as attempts were made
to understand the way in which past experiences influenced
current behaviour. These influences are seen as stemming
from the various psychological hungers an individual has
to satisfy if he is to develop emotionally. Behaviour is
seen as an attempt to satisfy these hungers by a variety
of means, depending on the way in which the impact and
influences of the past affect the present.

At birth, a baby has two types of need that must be
fulfilled if he is to survive and thrive: the need for
food and warmth to ensure physical survival, and the need
for physical and emotional contact with others for
emotional survival and development. Because the need for
food is manifested by hunger, the need for physical and
emotional contact is also described, within transactional
analysis, as a hunger. It is known as stimulus hunger
and is met by the physical contact and recognition that
babies receive in the form of cuddling and holding. This
is subsumed, in transactional analysis, under the concept
of strokes. As a child grows, such physical contact
normally decreases, and stimulus hunger comes to be
replaced by recognition hunger. This hunger can still be
met by physical contact, but it also includes other types
of stimuli, such as smiles, nods of recognition or
greetings. Thus, any transaction which results in
recognition of a person's existence becomes, along with
hugging, cuddling and other physical contact, the means

through which recognition hunger is satisfied. As with
stimulus hunger, the ways in which this hunger is met are
all subsumed under the concept of strokes.

STROKES IN TRANSACTIONAL ANALYSIS

Strokes can be helpful, enhancing emotional growth, or
unhelpful and restrictive. They can be unconditional
and related to 'being', or conditional and related to
'doing'. 'I love you', said with a smile or a hug is a
helpful, unconditional stroke, as it does not attach
conditions to being loved. 'You look attractive when you
wear blue' is a helpful, but conditional stroke as it
attaches certain conditions to looking attractive.
'You're stupid' is an unhelpful, unconditional stroke,
as it does not limit the area of stupidity to specific
aspects of behaviour. 'You're stupid when you cry' is
unhelpful as it can result in a child developing unhappy
feelings about himself, but conditional as it limits the
area of alleged stupidity (Woollams et al., 1976).

Strokes are only helpful if both verbal and non-verbal
aspects are congruent, and if they genuinely enhance
wellbeing. Giving someone a perfunctory peck on the
cheek whilst reading a newspaper over his shoulder is
not really a helpful stroke! Helpful conditional strokes
are a necessary and important part of the process of
socialization as they act to set appropriate limits on
behaviour, whereas unhelpful strokes usually set over-
restrictive limits. Babies who do not receive any kind
of stroking fail to thrive and may even die. People who
receive mainly unhelpful strokes as children may not
learn how to attract, accept or respond to helpful ones.
Because human beings can rarely tolerate the existential
vacuum occurring in the absence of strokes, such people
will seek out strokes similar to the ones received in
childhood, which at least confirm their existence, rather
than surviving without strokes at all.

Strokes can be given from, and received by, any of the
ego states in people. Carefully choosing and wrapping a
gift for someone who is ill is a stroke from the Parent;
being congratulated on a clear, concise and helpful
report is a stroke from the Adult; enjoying dancing with
a partner provides strokes for the Child in both individuals.

There are four major aspects to people's concern with

strokes. These are their willingness and ability to
accept, give, ask for and reject strokes. People whose
childhood experiences were generally constructive are
able to give strokes, usually helpful ones, generously
and appropriately. They can accept strokes from others
if they think they are accurate, but reject unwanted ones.
If they require strokes they are not afraid to ask others
for them. On the other hand, people who have had
destructive experiences as children may fear giving
helpful strokes, in case of rejection, although they may
give unhelpful ones, which serve to keep others at a
distance. When they are given helpful strokes, they may
reject, ignore or redefine them, but accept all the
unhelpful strokes they are given. Finally, they may seek
out unhelpful strokes from others (Steiner, 1974).

Strokes can range from those giving minimum recognition
to those providing emotional nourishment and enhancement.
Whilst the latter are essential, it can be all too easy
to ignore and under-value less intense 'maintenance'
strokes. The greeting by the postman, chat about the
weather or cricket with a shopkeeper, neighbourly gossip
or an interesting conversation with a stranger can enhance
the other, more intense strokes received in intimate
relationships. Such relationships might well become
claustrophobic if they were seen as the only authentic
way of receiving recognition from other people.

The impact that strokes have on individuals varies
according to their timing, source, intensity and
consistency. Strokes given early in life are likely to
have the most powerful impact on the recipients. Grown-
ups can use their Adult and Parent ego states to protect
themselves from unwanted or inappropriate strokes but
small children are unable to use any such protective
mechanism. Early unhelpful strokes, in particular, can
have a lasting and often destructive influence on
individuals. Strokes from people seen by individuals as
important to them are likely to have most impact. In
early childhood, parents are normally the major influence
although in later life relatives, teachers and friends
play a large part in providing strokes.

Small children usually receive a mixture of helpful
and unhelpful strokes, with helpful ones predominating in
families where the environment is stable and happy.
Despite this, it is suggested in transactional analysis
literature that, because the intensity of unhelpful
strokes is greater than that of helpful ones, the impact

of such strokes can be particularly powerful (Woollams and
Brown, 1979). My own experience in using transactional
analysis in teaching and counselling confirms this view.
I find that people who are relatively free of problems
and who have had mainly helpful stroking as children
nevertheless recall unhelpful strokes far more readily.
They usually recognise that they did, and still do,
receive many helpful strokes but they often have difficulty
in accepting these as readily as unhelpful ones or, indeed,
in accepting them at all.

For people who are using transactional analysis to help
themselves solve problems, their perception of past and
present stroking patterns is usually one in which
unhelpful stroking patterns predominate, with helpful
strokes being ignored, rejected or redefined. Ella has
a long history of depressive illnesses, which have been
little helped by medication and hospitalisation. She has
vivid and painful memories of a childhood in which she
felt unwanted, in which she was seen, in comparison with
her brother, as stupid, and in which her 'crossed eyes'
left her feeling, even after corrective treatment, ugly
and unattractive. As a result, Ella believes that she is
of little value, and she reinforces this belief by
rejecting and redefining helpful strokes she receives
from others, giving herself a constant barrage of unhelpful strokes and accepting any unhelpful ones that
come her way.

The kinds of strokes children receive and their
responses are crucial factors in the early decisions
they make about themselves and others, and their
subsequent script or life plan. Stroking which is
consistent and repeated is gradually incorporated into
individual frames of reference and later strokes sought
out, given and responded to in order to enhance and
reinforce these. Fay was a lively, extrovert member of
a transactional analysis therapy group. Highly
successful in her career, she was known as a charismatic
person who was always the 'life and soul' of any
situation. In the group it emerged that Fay had, as a
child, only received strokes and attention from her
father when she was being his pretty little girl, amusing
him by dancing and acting for him. As a result, Fay had
incorporated a message into her Parent ego state that,
to be liked, she had to perform for others. As an adult,
although she often longed to be the quiet member of a
committee meeting or to sit in a corner at a party,
talking to people she liked, she felt bound to continue

her performing role, fearing that, if she changed, she would
no longer receive recognition and attention from others.
Fay wanted to use group therapy to discover new ways of
behaving which enabled her to get strokes and attention for
other kinds of behaviour, with which she would feel more
comfortable and autonomous.

The emphasis in transactional analysis on the importance
and value of strokes from others tends to obscure and
devalue the strokes individuals can give themselves. The
literature suggests that such strokes can only occur in
the overall context of consistent stroking from others,
as internal strokes are said to draw on the reservoir of
strokes originally received from others. However, this
seems to be too narrow and limited a view. Whilst not
under-valuing the richness that can and does occur in
relationships between people, we perhaps have much to
learn from philosophies which emphasise the spiritual and
emotional growth that can come from within a person,
independently of his relationships with others. Perhaps
true autonomy can only occur when people are as comfortable
with themselves as they are with others, giving themselves
strokes which do not necessarily depend on receiving
strokes from others and which enhance emotional growth as
much as the strokes they receive from other sources.
Without this ability to feel secure with oneself, there is
a risk that individuals may feel that they only exist
through other people, with the result that they will
constantly seek out strokes from others to confirm their
existence, rather than to enhance their autonomy (Holloway,
in Barnes, ed., 1977).

STRUCTURE HUNGER AND TIME STRUCTURING

Transactional analysis theory suggests that each person
has to resolve for himself the existential dilemma of how
to structure his time between birth and death. The
discomfort many people feel when they find themselves with
unstructured time is called structure hunger. This third
hunger is seen as an extension of stimulus and recognition
hunger, as it also provides individuals with strokes. The
stroking pattern children receive in early childhood
influences their early decisions, and their views about
themselves and others. When people grow up, they continue
to seek out and give similar strokes to those they
received and gave in childhood, by structuring time and
relationships with others in ways which provide familiar
strokes and which also serve to reinforce early decisions.

Berne divided the ways in which individuals might spend their waking time into six categories. These are withdrawal, rituals, pastimes, activities, games and intimacy. The number and range of strokes available to individuals increase as they move from withdrawal through to intimacy. Thus, the quantity and quality of strokes received by people seems to vary according to the amount or proportion of their time in each of the categories given. Figure 4.1 gives two examples of time structuring, in which Y gets few strokes, whilst Z gets a large number.

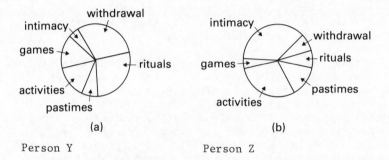

(a)   (b)

Person Y   Person Z

FIGURE 4.1   Two examples of time structuring

Withdrawal may be physical, as when a person is alone, or mental, as when someone withdraws into his own inner thoughts or fantasies whilst with other people. Although withdrawal does not provide an individual with strokes from others, it can be a very constructive way of spending time. Physical withdrawal can provide an opportunity for taking stock, recharging oneself, relaxing, or using time in creative ways, such as listening to music. Mental withdrawal can provide release from involvement in the boring parts of meetings, discussions or lectures, as well as providing an opportunity for idle and creative day-dreams and fantasies. Conversely, for someone who has an unhappy view of himself or others, withdrawal from relationships can provide a way of maintaining this view. Withdrawing from others can seem emotionally safe, as it avoids any possibility of being hurt or of having life positions and script-influenced behaviour challenged. Thus dysfunctional kinds of withdrawal reinforce unfulfilled, unhappy life styles and can, at their worst, result in mental breakdown and even suicide.

Rituals consist of predictable, stereotyped transactions about which there are known and widely accepted conventions. They provide a useful source of strokes, although they are at a fairly superficial 'maintenance' level. They can be important in providing individuals with a sense of belonging, either socially, geographically, culturally or religiously, and they are particularly useful in helping people to maintain a sense of 'self' when they are in new environments, and without their normal family and friendship network. Conversely, those individuals who fear close and authentic relationships with others may use rituals in order to keep other people at a safe emotional distance. When this occurs rituals, like withdrawal, can be unhelpful, reinforcing restrictive, unfulfilled and unhappy life styles.

Pastimes occur when people simply talk about things. The topics are usually safe ones, in which a degree of consensus or predictable levels of disagreement, can be expected. Berne gave pithy and vivid names to some typical pastimes. Wardrobe consists of discussions about clothes, fashion and cosmetics; General Motors of discussions about cars; in Ain't It Awful, people complain about things, ranging from grumbles about the weather, to complaints about levels of inflation, the youth of today and government policies. Pastimes are particularly useful in new encounters with people. They provide opportunities for testing out the interests, attitudes and values of others, and for evaluating the chances of new relationships becoming deeper and more intimate. In situations where people may not necessarily come together from choice, such as at work, as patients in hospital, or in meetings and parties, pastimes can act as useful social lubricants. They enable people who have little in common with each other to get on in a pleasant, if relatively superficial manner. Whilst pastiming may not, in itself, be of the same depth and richness as intimacy, it can be a pleasant and enjoyable way of transacting with others, and can provide a rich source of strokes. However, as with withdrawal and rituals, if pastiming is used to ensure that all relationships stay at a superficial level, it can be a restrictive way of spending time, and one which does not enhance the development of autonomy in individuals.

Activities deal with the demands of the external world, and are often subsumed under the heading of work although, in this context, the word has a wider application. Earning a living, cleaning the house, shopping, washing

clothes, cooking and do-it-yourself hobbies are all
examples of activities. The quantity and quality of
strokes provided by activities vary enormously from one
person to another. In shared activities, such as a team
work project, there may be a good deal of mutual giving
and accepting of strokes; someone cooking a meal may
give himself a stroke when he tastes it and looks at a
pleasantly set table and then receives strokes from
friends enjoying the meal he has cooked; a scientist who
works alone may give himself strokes, but not receive
strokes from others unless he produces some results from
his work. People tend to choose activities which fit
into their life position and script. People who are able
to enjoy their own company as well as rewarding relationships with others, will engage in a variety of activities,
which provide them with strokes, as well as receiving
strokes from others. Conversely, people who find it
difficult to give and receive strokes will choose
activities in which they can withdraw from contact with
others or, at most, engage in superficial, stereotyped
transactions which reinforce unfulfilled life styles.

Games are characterized by series of ambiguous, double-
level messages and are used to maintain superficial, non-
authentic and emotionally dishonest relationships, although
they may have the appearance of being loving and close.
Games analysis is a major part of transactional analysis
theory and it is dealt with separately in Chapter 5.

Intimacy is characterized by openness, authenticity
and honesty. Relationships based on intimacy are capable
of providing a rich and fulfilling source of helpful
strokes and of enhancing emotional growth and personal
fulfillment. People who have had destructive parenting
in their early years and who grow up without a capacity
for achieving intimacy with others often lead unhappy,
unsuccessful lives, in which they use games and other
superficial ways of structuring time in their relationships with others.

People tend to choose ways of structuring their time
in order to continue getting the kind of recognition and
strokes they received as children, thus reinforcing the
early decisions, life positions and scripts they
developed as a result of their own unique stroking
pattern. Guy was, as a child, given messages such as
'don't show your feelings', 'don't trust people' and
'work hard'. Demonstrations of affection were discouraged,
and he grew up feeling sad and depressed, wanting to make

close relationships, but without the skills and
permissions to do so. Guy worked hard at school
(activity), achieving academic success well beyond that
of his own parents. He was discouraged from making
friends at school and he isolated himself from his
contempories (withdrawal). As an adult with a successful
career, he found it difficult to make friends with
colleagues and, even outside work, his social contacts
were superficial and his interests solitary ones (activities, pastimes and rituals). He tried hard to make close
relationships with women, but his gaucheness, depressed
manner and efforts to make them feel sorry for him (games)
always ended in him being rejected. Guy's early decision,
that it was unwise to show feelings and to trust people,
was thus reinforced. Rather than find ways of resolving
his problems, Guy merely continued to work hard, to fail
in relationships and to feel depressed and unhappy (script
reinforcement).

There are a number of problems within transactional
analysis relating to the various hypotheses about time
structuring. The first concerns the concepts relating to
intimacy. Intimacy is clearly viewed as the most
constructive and fulfilling way of structuring time, yet
Berne and others argue that it occurs only rarely and
that when it does it is of brief duration. It is also
suggested that, even though intimacy is not confined to
sexual behaviour, it most usually occurs in relationships
where there is both a sexual and emotional component.
These views seem to narrow the concept of intimacy in a
way that is unhelpful and which reinforces the pessimistic,
determinist thread found in much of Berne's writings.
This narrow view of intimacy is compounded by the fact
that there is, I would suggest, an insufficient distinction
within the theory relating to time structuring between the
range of ways in which time can be spent, and the choice
of styles people can choose in relating to others! My own
view is that the range of ways can be subsumed under the
categories described, whilst the choice of styles can be
either games playing or authentic. When time structuring
is expanded to include range and style, individuals can
decide that they prefer to be authentic when relating to
others, regardless of the way in which they are structuring
their time.

Others may or may not respond in a similar fashion, but
this does provide people who choose an authentic style the
opportunity for developing intimacy within rituals,
pastimes and activities. They can thus reduce the level

of superficiality and increase the possibility for intimacy in aspects of time structuring which inevitably take up a good deal of our daily lives. Conversely, people who normally use games as a style of relating will do so within rituals, pastimes and activities, thus reducing their potential for close and intimate relation-ships. This extension to Berne's categories of time structuring seems to be rather closer to most people's experience, as it allows for a more complex, and richer pattern of behaviour. It is also a more optimistic approach, as it potentially enables people to spend a good deal of their time in intimacy in a variety of situations and relationships, rather than, as the literature suggests, enjoying it as a rare and very fleeting phenomenon. The implication of the view of intimacy as a rare event, is that most transactions must, if they are not intimate, be superficial and even dis-honest, whereas this revised model enables most transactions to be open and authentic.

This revision of the ideas relating to intimacy would also solve the second dilemma which arises from the views expressed in the literature. Intimacy is said by several writers to require more openness and honesty than most people are capable of, or can bear, and it is also said to make people vulnerable, as it opens them to the possibility of being hurt and rejected by others. This seems to imply that there is an expectation, covert or overt, that if one is open to others, a similar response is expected from them. However, genuine openness to others can only imply that people have made a decision about their own behaviour. It cannot assume a reciprocity of behaviour. If the ideas relating to styles of relating discussed earlier are accepted, this issue is easily resolved, as people can choose to adopt an authentic style of behaviour, regardless of the response they receive from others.

A third issue arises from the hierarchical approach to time structuring in which strokes range from zero (withdrawal) to unlimited (intimacy). It is clearly unrealistic and indeed inappropriate to be in a relation-ship of intimacy with every individual with whom one comes into contact, yet the hierarchical structure can seem to imply that ways of structuring time, other than through intimacy, are second-rate or second-best. My own view is that all ways of structuring time, other than through games, are potentially constructive and enhancing. The important factor is not so much how a

person spends his time, but how he relates to himself and
others within the structure he works out for himself
(Holloway in Barnes, ed., 1977).

Since people can use either an authentic or games
playing style of relating within rituals, pastimes and
activities, the way in which time is structured will
depend both on the choices they make about how to spend
their time and the style they use within these choices.
People who are autonomous will probably use intimacy as
a style of relating and will, as far as possible, avoid
dysfunctional levels of withdrawal or spending excessive
amounts of time in rituals, pastimes or games.

Chapter 5

The theory of games

Berne's best-known book 'Games People Play' (1967)
introduced games theory to a very wide audience. In
many ways this thesaurus of games did a disservice to
transactional analysis, as many people tended to see
games and transactional analysis as synonymous, rather
than seeing games analysis in context as a part of a
wider psychological model. In introducing the concept
of games, Berne used the word with a rather specialized
meaning. Other writers, notably Karpman (1968) and
Schiff (1975) have developed Berne's early concepts to
include an analysis of the roles people take on and the
symbiotic relationships they seek to establish when
playing games.

    The rationale for games originates in early childhood,
when children learn, through the kind of strokes they
receive, how to get attention and how to conform to
others' expectations of them. In families where parents
are generally autonomous and games-free, children receive
a variety of helpful and constructive strokes and are
encouraged to develop a flexible range of responses to
situations. As grown-ups, they are able to continue
responding to others and their environment in a constructive way, thus leading fulfilled lives which are
relatively free of games. In families where transactions
are ulterior, relationships lack intimacy and the strokes
given are unhelpful and destructive, children discover
that their natural responses to situations fail to meet
parental approval. In order to obtain strokes, they
learn to set repressive and destructive limits on their
feelings and behaviour. This process involves the
discounting or ignoring of some aspect of their Child
needs and, later, their Adult thinking and Parent nurturing
and guidance. It also leads to unhelpful decisions which

influence life positions and scripts in a restrictive and
sometimes destructive manner in adult life.

Adults who have made early decisions to repress the
existence or expression of certain feelings and behaviour
respond to situations in stereotyped and inappropriate
ways in order to reinforce these, using rackets and games
to get the attention they need and the strokes, however
unhelpful, with which they are familiar.

RACKETS IN TRANSACTIONAL ANALYSIS

The process by which a person manipulates other people in
order to confirm early decisions is called a racket,
whilst the feelings involved in manipulative or destructive
behaviour are called racket feelings. These feelings can
be internally or externally expressed. For example,
someone who refuses all invitations to go out and then
sits at home feeling sorry for himself is involved in
internal racket feelings. If he decides to go out to
dinner, but thinks he is only invited because people feel
sorry for him and he then behaves in a defensive and surly
manner, he is involved in an external expression of racket
feelings. Even though they are indirect, manipulative
ways of getting attention, the use of rackets can give
people the attention they want. When this fails, people
may move onto games in order to get the strokes and
attention they need from others (English, 1971 and 1972).

Racket feelings originate quite early in childhood and
usually come from the Adapted Child ego state. Once
developed, they become automatic reactions to situations,
regardless of their appropriateness. It is possible to
discover whether a particular emotion is a racket feeling
by asking the following questions:

1 is it repetitive, with the same feeling being used
   over and over again, in a variety of situations?;
2 is it inappropriate for the situation in which it
   is being used?;
3 is it a substitute, masking the expression of more
   authentic feelings?;
4 does it manipulate others into doing something for
   the person expressing the feeling? (Reddy, 1979).

If the answer to any or all of these questions is
affirmative, a racket feeling is normally being indulged.
Finally, it is important to ask whether the feeling leads

to effective problem solving. For example, authentic and appropriate anger can lead to effective action, whereas racket anger unfairly blames others for problems and may result in inappropriate action, or no action at all. The following example illustrates racket feelings occurring outside the context of a game. A social worker who uses anger as an automatic, racket response to situations is reprimanded by his team leader for failing to keep his records reasonably up to date. He responds with anger, but makes no attempt to resolve the problem. Instead, he remains angry all day, blaming the bureaucratic system, the secretaries and the team leader for his own inability to keep abreast of his recording. When he goes home, he does not explain the reason for his anger to his wife, but vents his feelings by criticizing the state of the house and the meal she has cooked. If his wife has learnt to use depression as a racket feeling, she will accept her husband's criticisms, however unjust, rather than seeking the real explanation for his anger. As their subsequent transactions continue, with racket feelings on his part and depression on hers, the couple may reach a point where they progress to a game.

GAMES IN TRANSACTIONAL ANALYSIS

A game is characterized by the following criteria:

(a)   it begins with a discount of some aspect of self or others which reinforces the early decision;

(b)   the process of a game involves the use of a variety of ulterior transactions, in which the social or verbal level is usually Adult - Adult, whilst the psychological or non-verbal level is usually Child - Child, Child - Parent, or Parent - Child;

(c)   the climax of the game occurs when there is a switch in the ego states being verbally expressed, and the hidden psychological level comes into the open;

(d)   at this stage, there is often a moment of confusion, before the participants end the game by indulging in racket feelings which serve to reinforce early decisions;

(e)   people are usually, though not always, unaware of the games they are playing.

Games can be played in any kind of situation, ranging from those in which people have only just met to those in which they are closely involved in long-term relation-

ships. Games are played in order to structure time and
to provide strokes, but as they also involve racket
feelings and ulterior transactions, they merely provide
an illusion of intimacy. They actually prevent the
development of real intimacy between people, but they do
offer temporary, if spurious relief from unhappy feelings
about self and others. They also enable people to
maintain a dysfunctional frame of reference, thus
providing a sense of security, making other people
predictable and reinforcing early decisions, life
positions and scripts. The following example illustrates
the process of a game. Henry is an elderly widower and
lives with his single daughter Jane, aged thirty. As a
child, Henry had his Adult thinking capacity and Parent
nurturing ability discounted and repressed by over-
protective parents. As a result, he had little ability
to look after his Free Child needs, or to think things
out clearly, and he learnt to use racket feelings and
behaviour of helplessness and depression in order to
continue being looked after by others and to reinforce
his own lack of autonomy. When Jane was young, she
modelled herself on her mother, who looked after Henry,
developing her Nurturing Parent in order to look after
her father, and repressing her own Free Child needs. Jane
learnt to use racket feelings of anger and resentment in
her relationships with others, in particular with her
father. A typical game between Henry and Jane might open
with the following transaction:

Henry:	sounding depressed and anxious.
Stimulus:	'You ought to go out and enjoy yourself. Don't worry about me - I'll be all right left on my own.'
Ego state:	(verbal) Adult - Adult information. (non-verbal) Child seeking Parent nurturing.
Jane:	sounding irritable and resentful.
Response:	'That's all right, Dad. I'm not a great one for going out. I'll stay in and keep you company.'
Ego state:	(verbal) Adult - Adult information. (non-verbal) Parent to Child.

These ulterior transactions continue, with Henry
suggesting people Jane might visit or things she could
do, and Jane denying her need for company or entertainment.
The switch occurs when Jane makes her father a cup of
tea which he spills over the carpet. Jane reacts with
anger, not only about the tea, but about her father's
general inability to look after himself and her lack of
a life of her own. At this point, the hidden non-verbal
level of the transaction comes into the open.

Henry:	sounding childlike.
Stimulus:	'Look what I've done - I am stupid.'
Ego state:	Child seeking Parent reaction.
Jane:	sounding angry and upset.
Response:	'Yes, you are - and I'm fed up with always looking after you and with never going out.'
Ego state:	Parent response to Child stimulus.

At this stage, Henry feels confused (I told her to go out) before switching into his racket feelings of depression and reminding himself of how helpless he is, whilst Jane indulges in her racket feelings of anger and resentment.

Although games can be infinitely varied, Berne gave pithy and succinct names to those he found to be most frequently used. As these have already been fully described in 'Games People Play', they will not be discussed in detail here, although one game will be presented as an illustration of game formulation. The game of Why Don't You, Yes But was the first to be named and was said by Berne to be the one most commonly played. Certainly, it is an all too familiar game in social work and counselling although, if it is to be played effectively, it requires a partner who will play I'm Only Trying To Help You. The game begins with A asking B for advice. At this point, A is discounting his own ability to work out solutions to problems. B responds 'why don't you....' and provides a possible solution to the problem, thus colluding with A's discount of his problem-solving ability. A responds to B's suggestion with 'yes, but....' followed by a reason for rejecting the advice. B goes on giving advice, with A continuing to reject it. The transactions are ulterior as, although the verbal level is Adult - Adult information-giving and seeking, the non-verbal level consists of A's Child seeking help from a position of helplessness and inadequacy, with B responding from a position of superiority, which reinforces A's feelings, rather than solving the problem. The switch occurs when A states that B's advice is useless and his problems are insoluble. B feels confused (I was only trying to help him) and rejected, whilst A feels racket anger or depression, and reinforces his position of helplessness. B also indulges in racket feelings of righteous indignation.

One way of recognising games is to use the following series of questions (James, J., 1973):

1 what keeps happening?
   The repetitive nature of behaviour usually
   indicates that games are being played in order to
   reinforce a particular frame of reference;
2 how does the pattern of behaviour start, continue
   and end?
   This identifies the name of the game as well as
   various aspects of the process, including the
   roles taken and the ego states involved;
3 how do the people involved in the game feel at the
   end?
   This identifies the racket feeling;
4 at the end of the game, what do they think about
   themselves and others?
   This identifies the life positions involved;
5 if people involved in the game behaved differently,
   what might be the outcome?
   This identifies the underlying, unmet needs which
   have been repressed and provides a clue to the
   authentic feelings and needs which have been masked
   by the game;
6 what could they do to change the game?
   This identifies whether there is any energy
   available for change and can act as a first step
   in breaking games, as it encourages a new look at
   behaviour.

Games can be played at various intensities, referred
to as degrees. Berne has identified three degrees of
intensity:
1 first degree games are socially acceptable to those
   involved in the participants' circle. Although
   they involve indirect ways of relating, they are
   relatively harmless;
2 second degree games are usually concealed from
   those who are not involved in the game, as they
   are not socially acceptable. They may be played
   until there has been, for example, withdrawal from
   a relationship;
3 third degree games are all-consuming and result in
   permanent physical or emotional damage, such as
   drug addiction, or alcoholism. At their most
   intense, they can occasionally end in homicide or
   suicide.

For example, in a marriage, a first degree game occurs
when a husband fails to tell his wife that he will be
late home from work. When he finally arrives, he finds
dinner is spoilt and his wife is angry. After a brief

quarrel, the couple solve their differences in an amicable
way and, most importantly, work out ways of avoiding a
similar situation in future. A second degree game occurs
when a couple have frequent, bitter and unresolved
arguments with each other. These are terminated in
temporary withdrawal from the relationship, refusing
intercourse, sleeping in separate rooms or going home to
mother, but not in attempts to solve the problems between
them. A third degree game occurs when a relationship is
characterized by emotional or physical abuse and violence.

ROLES IN GAMES

Karpman's analysis of the roles that people take on when
playing games provides another dimension to games theory.
He suggests that games are played from one of three roles
or positions. A Persecutor is over-critical and authoritarian, setting unnecessary limits on others' behaviour.
A Rescuer, in the guise of helping others, actually
encourages their dependency. A Victim sees himself as
unjustly discriminated against, and blames others for
his problems as well as failing to take responsibility
for his own behaviour. Persecuting usually comes from
the Controlling Parent ego state; Rescuing from the
Nurturing Parent; and Victim behaviour from the Adapted
Child. In the course of a game, the participants may
switch roles on one or more occasions, ending the game
in a role which fits in with their racket feelings and
early decisions. This is shown graphically by the drama
triangle (see Figure 5.1).

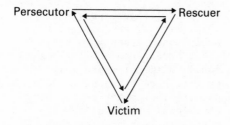

FIGURE 5.1 Drama triangle showing roles played in games

The drama triangle can be used to identify the roles
in the game played by Henry and Jane. When the game
begins, Henry is the Victim being rescued by Jane. When

the switch occurs, Jane becomes a Persecutor. If the
game continues, with Henry telling Jane how much he has
done for her over the years and accusing her of ingrati-
tude, he becomes the Persecutor and Jane becomes the
Victim. If Jane bursts into tears in response to her
father's accusations, Henry might switch to Rescuer and
comfort her, apologising for his churlish behaviour.
At this point, with Henry rescuing Jane who remains a
Victim, the game might end, at least for the time being.

SYMBIOSIS IN GAMES

Symbiosis occurs when two people behave as if, between
them, they formed only one person with neither person
utilizing a full range of ego states. Symbiotic
relationships originate in childhood. Normally parents
encourage the development of all three ego states in
their children, thus enabling them, when they grow up,
to use all their ego states in relationships with
others. However, in some families, parents may behave
in such a way that symbiotic relationships develop
between them and their children. Parents may repress
the Child needs in their children and force the development of the Parent and Adult because they want their own
Child needs looked after. Alternatively, parents may
repress the development of the Adult and Parent in their
children, thus keeping them in a dependent situation.
A child who grows up in either of these situations fails
to develop effective use of all his ego states and, as
an adult, he seeks to recreate the original symbiosis
through playing games.

When people develop symbiotic relationships with each
other, they can be either complementary or competitive.
In a complementary relationship, one person with a
functional Parent and Adult but a repressed Child looks
after another with a functional Child but repressed
Adult and Parent. In a competitive relationship, the
people involved either compete to look after each other,
in which case both lack a functional Child, or seek to
be looked after, in which case both lack a functional
Adult and Parent. In the relationship between Henry and
Jane, the symbiosis is basically a complementary one, with
Jane looking after Henry, although when the 'switch' in
the game occurs, Jane, temporarily at least, competes to
be looked after.

Symbiotic relationships are established and maintained

by discounting an aspect of self, others or external
reality. Four kinds of discounting have been identified
(Schiff, 1975). The existence of the problem can be
discounted. For example, a letter from the bank about
an overdrawn account is torn up and the problem denied
by ignoring it. The significance of the problem can be
discounted. The problem is acknowledged but not seen as
important. 'After all, everyone's in debt, what's the
point of trying to keep in credit when there's so much
inflation?' The possibility of change can be discounted.
Here, the problem is seen as important, but no solutions
seem to be available. 'I am worried, but it's not my
fault. I blame inflation.' Finally, the personal
abilities of the person with the problem are discounted.
The problem is seen as important and the person takes
responsibility for it, but cannot see any way he can
solve it. 'I can't work any harder, or cut down on my
expenses, so there's nothing I can do about it.' When
people use discounting as a mechanism, they fail to use
all their ego states effectively, but instead seek out
others who either solve the problem for them, or collude
with their helplessness.

AN INTEGRATED APPROACH TO GAMES

The various aspects of games theory developed by different
writers can be integrated to provide a single, unified
concept relating to games. Small children who have
aspects of their personality repressed, or developed too
rapidly, learn to discount feelings, thinking or their
potential for nurturing. They then make unhelpful
decisions about their life positions, scripts and frames
of reference. In later life, the process by which they
manipulate situations in order to confirm these early
decisions are rackets, and the emotions connected with
these are racket feelings. Symbiotic relationships are
established and games, using series of ulterior transactions, are played from various roles in order to
maintain the symbiotic relationship, and to reinforce
early decisions, life positions, and scripts. The
external world is 'filtered' through each person's unique
frame of reference in such a way that it fits into and
reinforces it (see Figure 5.2).

According to transactional analysis literature, a
good deal of the time in people's lives and relationships,
particularly those which are emotionally intense, such
as marriage, is said to be based on games rather than

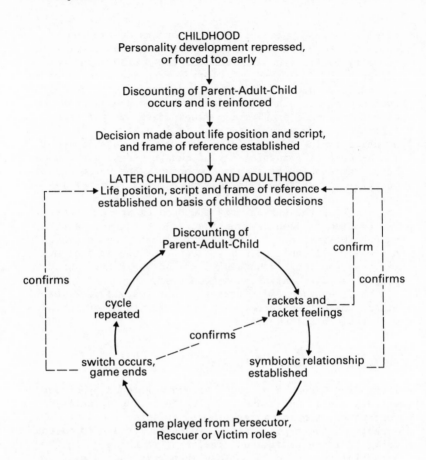

FIGURE 5.2   An integrated approach to games

intimacy. Games are said to be played because people
know of no other way of relating. Everyone is said to
need games as part of their time structuring. First
degree games are seen as relatively harmless, and indeed
some games are seen as constructive rather than destructive ways of spending time. However, these views seem
to contradict others widely held within transactional
analysis, in which games are seen as indirect, inauthentic
ways of meeting needs and getting strokes, and as ways of
preventing intimacy between people. If this is so, then
games, at whatever level, seem to be unhelpful ways of
structuring time. This dilemma is resolved if the
revised framework for time structuring is used (as
suggested in Chapter 4), as this involves both a range
and style of relating to others. In this case, people

can choose to avoid games as a style of relating to
others and can instead choose authenticity in their time
structuring and relationships with others.

Chapter 6

The theory of scripts

It has already been explained that much of a child's
early experience consists of strokes, or units of
recognition, from parents and significant others. It
is the nature of these strokes which determines a child's
life position or view of himself and others. Strokes
are passed to a child in the form of verbal and non-
verbal messages, which tell him how he is perceived by
others and how he is expected to think, feel and behave
in order to fit acceptably within his own family. These
messages form the basis of the child's life plan or
script, as they tell him how to live out his life. The
life position taken and the type of script developed by
a child depends on the decisions he makes in response to
parental messages.

MAKING DECISIONS

The age at which decisions are made varies according to
a child's family situation. A child whose autonomy and
emotional development are adversely affected by destructive strokes and messages is liable to make decisions
when very young which, although they meet parental
expectations at the time, are ultimately dysfunctional
for him. These decisions result, as he grows up, in a
rigid, closed frame of reference and non-autonomous
behaviour. This serves to reinforce the early decisions
and to confirm an individual in his view about himself
and others. Much apparently dysfunctional behaviour in
older children and adults makes sense when viewed in
the context of the messages they received and decisions
they made in early childhood. Unhelpful and destructive
decisions are usually made before the Adult and Parent
ego states have fully developed. These messages are

incorporated into the Child ego state and act as unhelpful
restrictions on the Free Child. The Child in the Child
(C_c) reacts with feelings, whilst the Adult in the Child
(A_c), in the interests of the child's acceptability within
the family, works out how to behave in order to get strokes
and to meet parental expectations. If this behaviour is
reinforced by parents and others, it becomes, in time, an
automatic response from the Parent in the Child (P_c),
regardless of its appropriateness in situations. As long
as behaviour fits into family expectations, the child can
get the strokes he needs. Problems arise as the child
grows up and tries to use this behaviour outside the
family, by seeking out situations and relationships which
enable him to behave in ways which fit in with his early
decisions. At this later stage, the dysfunctional aspect
of these early decisions often becomes apparent.

Ella provides an example of the way in which early
decisions can be dysfunctional in later life. Ella was
referred because of her persistent feelings of depression,
sadness, worthlessness and inadequacy. Her behaviour
reflected her inner confusion and depression. She was
weepy, lethargic and bored, unable to enjoy herself, her
family or friendships and unable to get on with tasks,
such as housework or making friends, which she felt she
wanted to do. She lacked both energy and ideas which
would help her to change her feelings, attitudes and
behaviour and felt that she had no choice but to continue
her life in a depressed and unhappy manner. Ella had
grown up in a family in which many members suffered
physical or mental illness and some even committed
suicide. Her mother spent all her time caring for a
permanently sick husband and Ella learnt, at an early
age, that the way to get attention was to need looking
after by being ill. She also learnt that girls were not
as clever as boys (a 'don't think' message); they did
what they were told, were passive, quiet and 'good'
(reinforcement of the 'don't think' message); they kept
the peace, did not show their feelings, particularly
those of anger or aggression (a 'don't show your feelings'
message). Although, as a child, Ella was given strokes
for being 'good', passive and conforming, as an adult
this kind of behaviour left her unable to think clearly,
to solve problems constructively or to look after her
own Child needs. Ella married a man who took on the
role of looking after her and who colluded with her
seeming inadequacy in various areas of her life. This
still did not give Ella the strokes she needed and she
continued the family pattern of getting strokes and

attention for being ill by being persistently depressed, spending several periods in hospital and having various kinds of therapy.

A child who grows up in an emotionally stable family and who receives mainly constructive strokes and messages, is likely to make decisions later, rather than earlier, and to develop a frame of reference in which he views himself and others positively. He is open to new ideas and information which may, on occasions, be relevant to his current situation but which conflict with the information on which earlier decisions were based. When this occurs, an individual with an open and flexible frame of reference can make new and more appropriate decisions. An example of this process occurring in the course of counselling is provided by Kate. Despite a history of stormy and unhappy relationships with men, Kate had, at the time she sought counselling help, established a loving, stable and happy relationship. However, she was aware that she often behaved in ways which put the relationship at risk and, as this conflicted with her desire to maintain it, she was rather puzzled by her own behaviour. We quickly discovered that Kate had received consistent messages from her mother about the general worthlessness of men. As Kate's parents were unhappily married and as her father left home when she was an adolescent, Kate believed that her mother's view was correct. Although many of her own early relationships with men served to reinforce this belief, Kate was aware that men and women did enjoy close and loving relationships with each other and she had, prior to seeing a counsellor, made some constructive changes in her own attitudes and beliefs, thus enabling her to establish a loving relationship. Counselling helped her to understand how her early internalized messages and subsequent decisions and beliefs about men might still be influencing her and these insights into her apparently contradictory and puzzling behaviour enabled her to change both her early decisions and her potentially destructive behaviour.

Five factors influence the impact that parental and other messages have on a child (Woollams and Brown, 1979). Firstly, a child lacks power in relation to the adults around him. He may feel fear, frustration, anger and terror when he is faced with intolerable discrepancies between his own ability, based on his size and strength at the time, and the demands and expectations of adults. If he is physically or emotionally threatened or abused,

he can do little to retaliate or to protect himself.
Secondly, a child's ability to understand, tolerate and
deal with stressful situations is also limited. When
faced with stress resulting from emotional or physical
abuse, he may become excessively anxious, frustrated,
withdrawn or angry. Thirdly, a small child's thinking
is primarily intuitive, rather than rational and logical,
and he may make faulty decisions on the basis of this
limited thinking capacity. Fourthly, a child often lacks
information and understanding about the situations in
which he finds himself and about which he may, on
occasions, need to make decisions. Finally, a child,
in contrast to most adults, lacks options about how to
change a situation he finds distressing or intolerable.
Most adults, on the other hand, can think rationally,
do have at least some information, and even when their
options are limited, do have some degree of choice about
how to respond to situations.

LIFE POSITIONS

A small child's early decisions usually result in him
taking up a basic life position, or view of himself and
others. The four basic positions are as follows:
  1 I'm O K - You're O K;
  2 I'm O K - You're not O K;
  3 I'm not O K - You're O K;
  4 I'm not O K - You're not O K.

When a child is born, he is assumed to be in the first
position, in which self and others are viewed positively.
In a newly-born baby, this is obviously not a consciously
articulated position. In an older child or adult, this
position is one in which a person 'gets on with life',
valuing himself and others, enjoying the ways in which
he spends his time, making close and loving relationships
with other people, learning from mistakes and dealing
constructively with the changes and problems which are
an inevitable part of life (Ernst, 1971). A person in
the first position normally uses his Helpful Free and
Adapted Child, and Helpful Controlling and Nurturing
Parent in dealing with situations and relationships. He
is generally games-free in his behaviour and authentic
in relationships with others.

Some writers suggest that the powerlessness of childhood results in all children moving into one of the other
three positions (Harris, 1973). In my view, this does not

seem to be borne out by observation. Many people lead
happy, constructive and fulfilled lives, dealing with
problems and setbacks from the first position, with any
shift into one of the other positions at times of stress
being only temporary. English (in Barnes, ed., 1977)
suggests that for adults, the position of 'I'm O K - You're
O K' involves a person in seeking autonomy for himself
and intimacy with others, whilst recognising the fallibility
of people, himself included. She sees this as a more
realistic and less idealised position and calls it 'I'm
O K - You're O K - Adult'.

For people whose adult lives are marred by problems
in which their own attitudes and behaviour play an
important part, there has usually been a decision to take
up one of the other three life positions. Whilst
behaviour, within any one of these positions, can range
from mildly to severely dysfunctional, the more serious
aspects are emphasised here in order to highlight the
differences between the positions.

The second position is often referred to as the
paranoid or 'get rid of' one, in which a person feels
persecuted or victimised by others. He denies his own
part in the problems he faces, refuses to accept any
responsibility for the consequences of his actions, and
may feel that the world owes him a living or that others
are thwarting him in achieving his potential or ambitions.
A person in this position uses mainly Unhelpful Controlling
and Nurturing Parent in dealing with situations. A common
game is If It Weren't For You, whilst relationships are
often based on a complementary Parent - Child symbiosis,
in which he is the victim. A person in this position is,
in fact, defending himself against internal feelings of
worthlessness, despair or depression by projecting his
fears onto others and a more accurate way of describing
this second position is 'I'm not O K (although I pretend
I am) - You're not O K' (Klein, 1980).

The third position is often referred to as the
depressive or 'get away from' one, in which a person sees
himself as depressed, inadequate, helpless or worthless
and others as competent, adequate and powerful. People
in this position are often overly compliant or passive,
blaming themselves entirely when things go wrong and
believing that they are unloveable. A person in this
position uses mainly Unhelpful Adapted Child and
Controlling Parent ego states in dealing with situations
and relationships. Common games are Poor Me and Wooden

Leg, whilst relationships are often based on a complementary
Child - Parent symbiosis, in which the person concerned
seeks someone to look after him, or to rescue him from his
victim role.

The fourth position is often referred to as the
futility or 'give up' one, in which a person sees both
himself and others as worthless and of no value. A
person in this position feels extreme despair, alienation
and hopelessness. He may abuse himself with alcohol or
drugs, end up in prison or mental hospital or even commit
suicide. A person in this position also uses mainly
Unhelpful Adapted Child and Controlling Parent in dealing
with situations. A common game is Yes, But, in which the
person concerned reinforces both his own and others'
supposed inadequacies. When relationships with others
are made, they are often based on a competitive symbiosis,
in which each person struggles unsuccessfully to get the
other to meet his needs.

A child who grows up in a very unhappy family situation
may move from the first position to one of the others in
relation to all aspects of his life. A child who grows
up in a relatively stable and happy home may remain in
the first position in relation to most situations but
move into one of the other positions in respect of
particular aspects of his life. For example, many women
still learn, despite the influence of the feminist
movement in society, to feel competent and comfortable
in their nurturing role of looking after others, but
move into one of the other three positions in terms of
their competence in situations, such as pursuing a career,
in which logical thinking and decision-making are
required. Conversely, many men feel comfortable when
using their Adult ego states in dealing with work situations, but move into one of the other positions when
they find themselves needing to use nurturing skills
or to respond affectively and intimately to others.

Once a child has taken up his basic life position,
he perceives and responds to situations and other people
in such a way that his chosen position is reinforced
and validated. Other than in the first position, this
usually means discounting or redefining some aspect of
his own feelings, others' behaviour or the situation.
Beth, for example, used to redefine transactions and
play Yes, But in order to put others 'on a pedestal' and
to maintain a position in which she felt not O K.

SCRIPT DEVELOPMENT

The decisions made by a person in childhood affect both
the content of his life and its process.   The content
depends on the way in which time and relationships with
others are structured, whilst the process depends on the
life plan or script a person adopts.   Both content and
process are influenced by the messages which are passed
to children by their parents and which are incorporated
into a child's life script.   These messages are sent in
three different ways: modelling, attributing and
suggesting (Woollams and Brown, 1979).   All three ways
are intended, as part of the process of socialization,
to influence a child's behaviour, feelings and attitudes.

   Parental behaviour often provides a model which can be
copied by children in their play, conversations and
relationships with each other.   Children absorbed in
playing with their dolls, banging nails into pieces of
wood, ordering their playmates about, confiding secrets
or cuddling a hurt pet may all be copying, in childish
fashion, the behaviour they have observed in their
parents.   This modelled and copied behaviour is gradually
integrated into the child's developing personality until
it becomes a natural part of his behaviour.

   Sometimes, a particular kind of behaviour is attributed
to a child.   'Little boys don't cry', given as a
consistent message to a child may result in his learning
to ignore or deny any physical or emotional pain in order
to maintain the behaviour attributed to him by the early
message.

   Sometimes, a child receives suggestions about how he
should behave.   These messages are often weaker in their
impact than those given by modelling or attributing.
Thus, 'it would be nice to have a doctor in the family'
merely acts as a suggestion about future behaviour,
whereas 'there's always been a doctor in the family' is
a much stronger directive.

   The impact of messages depends on their intensity,
source, frequency, consistency and type.   Messages from
parents which are consistent, repeated frequently and
given in the form of destructive, unhelpful strokes are
liable to have a far more powerful impact on a child
than the occasional constructive strokes from a busy
teacher or relative.

The following discussion, which looks at the way in which messages are received by children, brings together two theoretical viewpoints, as this seems to me to cover the different stages of child development more completely than either viewpoint on its own. Messages which are constructive and which encourage the development of autonomy and intimacy are known as permissions, whilst those which have an unhelpful or repressive impact on the personality are known as injunctions and drivers (Woollams and Brown, 1979). Early messages are passed from the three primary ego states of the parents to the Child ego state of the infant (Woollams and Brown, 1979). When all three primary ego states have developed in the infant, later messages pass to all these ego states (Steiner, 1971) (see Figure 6.1).

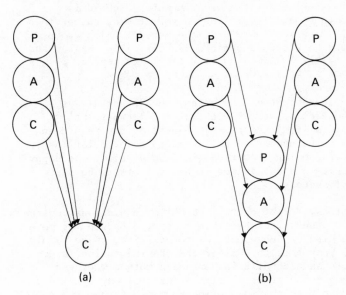

(a)   (b)

early childhood   later childhood
FIGURE 6.1   A script matrix

Script theory, to date, has tended to concentrate more on the unhelpful and restrictive messages that children receive from their parents. As a result, it is the ideas relating to injunctions and drivers rather than permissions that have been most fully developed, although this balance has been altered recently with the work done by Gere (1975) and Goulding and Goulding (1976). Even though children are rarely given injunctions, drivers and permissions in brief and succinct terms, such as 'don't think', 'don't feel', 'be happy', or

'trust people', it is normally possible to use such
phrases to summarize very accurately the meanings and
intentions of parental messages.

The injunctions, or unhelpful messages from the
Child of the parents to the Child of the infant, are
usually stated as 'don'ts', e.g. 'don't be close', 'don't
think', or 'don't show your feelings'. The drivers, or
unhelpful messages from the Parent of the parents go to
the Child of the infant before the development of his
primary Parent. When the primary Parent ego state of
the infant has developed, parents pass driver messages
from their Parent to the Parent ego state in the infant.
These messages are usually stated as 'do's' and concern
parental values about the ways in which a child is
expected to behave, e.g. 'look after others, rather than
yourself', or 'work hard and make money'. Five groups
of drivers have been described (Kahler, 1974, Kahler and
Hedges, 1975). These are 'try hard', 'be perfect',
'please me', 'be strong' and 'hurry up'.

Drivers and injunctions often, though not always,
reinforce each other. For example, a 'be perfect'
driver and a 'don't be close' injunction may result in
a person being unable to relax and to enjoy relationships
with others, being a 'workoholic', only able to be happy
when working and succeeding in his efforts to be a
financial success.

Sometimes, Parent driver and Child injunctions contradict each other, and when this occurs, a person may move
from one kind of behaviour to another kind, as he vainly
tries to obey both the driver and the injunction, e.g. a
child with an alcoholic father and a mother who over-
protects him and regards drink as an evil may receive a
'drink, don't think' injunction from his father and a
'stay sober and please me' driver from his mother. As
a result, his behaviour might alternate between alcoholic
bingeing and 'going on the waggon'.

The contradictions and conflicts which a person may
experience between the script messages received by his
Child and those received by his Parent may arise from
several sources. Sometimes, parents pass different
messages to the child as he grows up, with the intention
of counteracting early ones; the child may receive
powerful messages from people outside the family which
contradict those received from his parents; sometimes,
an adult may re-evaluate the messages he has received as

a child, and make new decisions about those which are giving rise to conflicts. Counselling can often be helpful in enabling people to identify and resolve the conflicts resulting from contradictory internalised messages.

An example of this kind of conflict was demonstrated by Lynn who, in a group setting, was working on a problem relating to her apparent need to make mistakes at work which resulted in her being reprimanded, but which seemed to conflict with her general level of competence and ability. Lynn felt that she could be as successful at work as she was in other areas of her life, but found she seemed driven to make mistakes. It emerged that, as a very young child, Lynn had internalized some unhelpful messages about failure as she was always compared unfavourably with her sister. Later, she had incorporated into her Adult and Parent ego states more constructive messages about how to be competent and how to nurture others successfully. It was confirmed by Lynn's husband that in the other areas of her life, she was able to be successful, competent and to learn from mistakes. Lynn had the ability to transfer this competence to work, yet she seemed instead to live out her early internalized messages about failing. As Lynn began to explore the contradictions between the earlier and later messages she had incorporated, she began to realize that she already had the necessary skills, knowledge and ability to succeed at work. She needed, however, to decide that the early messages about failing were no longer appropriate or necessary to her and to transfer her general ability to succeed in her work situation (Pitman, 1981).

The Adult ego state of the parents shows the child how to carry out the behaviour which results from the child's internalization of script drivers and injunctions. A woman with a 'hurry up' driver and a 'don't be close' injunction may pass these onto her child by discouraging the expression of affection, being obsessively houseproud, and being too harrassed and busy to enjoy her husband's or child's company.

Early permissions which encourage the autonomy of the child and his emotional growth and development are, like injunctions and drivers, passed to the Child ego state. Later permissions pass to all three primary ego states. These messages come mainly from the Helpful parts of the parents' Nurturing and Controlling Parent, Adult and Helpful Free and Adapted Child ego states.

In the process of growing up, a child needs eight permissions in order to develop his autonomy (Goulding and Goulding, 1976). If the child receives restrictive injunctions instead, his emotional growth and autonomy are stunted and warped. The permissions and their corresponding injunctions are given in a developmental order, corresponding to the chronological development and needs of the child. They are as follows:

1 to exist: given when a child is loved and valued and given good physical and emotional nurturing. An unwanted child who is abused and neglected from birth onwards receives instead a 'don't exist' injunction;

2 to have and be aware of sensations: given when a child has parents who are relaxed about his bodily functions, and who encourage his exploration of the world around him. A child whose parents are obsessive about or embarrassed by the child's bodily functions or who discourage his exploration of the environment receives a 'don't feel sensations' injunction;

3 to feel emotions: given when a child's spontaneous expression of happiness, affection, or sadness are accepted by his parents. A child who is discouraged from expressing his feelings spontaneously or who is only allowed to express a narrow range of feelings, regardless of their appropriateness in situations, receives a 'don't feel' injunction;

4 to think: given when parents respond constructively to a child's exploration of and questioning about the world around him. A child whose thinking ability is ignored, discounted, made fun of or criticized, receives a 'don't think' injunction;

5 to be emotionally and physically close to others: given when a child receives relaxed and consistent nurturing and emotional care. A child who is abused, ignored or discouraged from trusting anyone, receives a 'don't be close' injunction;

6 to be who you are: given when a child's particular physical attributes and blend of talents and abilities are encouraged by his parents. A child who is teased about his appearance, or who is made to respond to parental expectations, rather than being encouraged to develop his own abilities, receives a 'don't be you' injunction;

7 to be one's age: given when parents allow a child to develop naturally, neither smothering his growth, nor forcing it too quickly. A child whose

development is forced too rapidly or who is over-
protected may receive a 'don't be your age'
injunction;

8 to succeed: given when a child's competence,
   skills and achievements are supported and encouraged
   by parents. A child who is over-protected and not
   encouraged to become competent, or whose achievements are discounted or ignored, receives a 'don't
   succeed' injunction.

The question of whether it is possible to be free of
the influences of parental and other messages and,
therefore, script-free is still being debated. However,
it seems unlikely that anyone is entirely free of script
influence, although some people clearly have constructive
scripts, which enable them to enjoy authenticity in their
relationships with others and to be flexible in their
behaviour.

There are three basic scripts: winning or constructive, non-winning or banal, and losing or tragic scripts
(Steiner, 1974). The first type is normally called
'winning' but I will use the word 'constructive' in the
following discussion, as it implies a co-operative,
rather than a competitive style of relating to others.

Individuals with constructive scripts are autonomous
and authentic in their relationships with others,
operating from an 'I'm O K - You're O K' life position.
Much of the literature within transactional analysis
describes constructive scripts in such glowing terms
that few ordinary mortals would seem to be capable of
aspiring to them! This is compounded by the emphasis
on banal and losing scripts and on the alleged inability
of people to achieve intimacy, other than fleetingly.
Whilst this emphasis is perhaps inevitable, as transactional analysis was developed from work with people
with emotional and behavioural problems, observation
and experience seem to me to suggest that many people,
whilst not as 'perfect' as the literature indicates,
do lead generally happy, fulfilled and rewarding lives,
which would seem to fit within the general framework of
a constructive script.

Banal scripts usually develop when people have
received a fairly equal mixture of constructive and
destructive or restrictive messages which, taken together,
discourage an exploration of potential and the development of autonomy, but which give some scope for getting

on with life and for enjoying at least the illusion of
success and contentment. Banal scripts are said to result
in people who are fearful of taking risks, and who settle
for the known, conformity and the predictable. They are
characterized by tedium, dullness and perhaps, for the
individuals concerned, occasional glimpses of what might
have been, and an awareness that their potential has in
some ways never been fully realized. Banal scripts have
been written about in detail by writers who take a
radical, political perspective in exploring what they
see as the damaging effects of cultural, sexual and social
scripting, and who conclude that the majority of people
develop banal, rather than constructive scripts (Steiner,
1974; Wyckhoff, ed., 1976).

Banal scripting is beautifully described in T.S. Eliot's
poem, 'The Love Song of J. Alfred Prufock' (1936).

No! I am not Prince Hamlet, nor was meant to be;
Am an attendant lord, one that will do
To swell a progress, start a scene or two,
Advise the prince; no doubt, an easy tool,
Deferential, glad to be of use,
Politic, cautious, and meticulous;
Full of high sentence, but a bit obtuse;
At times, indeed, almost ridiculous -
Almost, at times, the Fool.

I grow old... I grow old...
I shall wear the bottoms of my trousers rolled.

Shall I part my hair behind? Do I dare to eat a peach?
I shall wear white flannel trousers, and walk upon the
    beach.
I have heard the mermaids singing, each to each.

I do not think that they will sing to me.

Although many people lead lives which may, to outsiders,
seem to be ordinary, uneventful and lacking in stimulus
and which therefore seem to fit in with descriptions of
banal scripting, it is important not to under-value the
personal strengths, autonomous characteristics and
richness of experience of those whose lives are generally
peaceful and undramatic. After all, J. Alfred Prufock
did hear the mermaids, even if he didn't think they would
sing to him!

People who receive mainly destructive or restrictive

messages from their parents and for whom the wider
environment is a hostile one, develop losing scripts of
varying degrees of severity and dysfunction. Adults with
such scripts would have grown up in families where their
parents used mainly unhelpful, rather than helpful, aspects
of their Adapted Child and Parent ego states, passing on
to their children feelings of anger, depression, guilt or
anxiety and being inconsistent, cruel, authoritarian or
neglectful in their handling. Such children would not
receive the permissions needed for emotional development,
and they would move into one of the 'not O K' life
positions, coming to believe that they cannot trust the
world to give them attention, love and security. They
would develop a script which is characterized by its
repetitive, dysfunctional nature. People with losing
scripts rarely make happy and fulfilled relationships.
They fail to learn from mistakes or to handle problems
constructively and never quite succeed at what they want
to achieve. They may become mentally ill or physically
abuse themselves, often ending up in mental hospital or
prison, or committing suicide or homicide.

Banal and losing scripts have been further sub-divided
into various themes. They can be categorized as 'never',
'always', 'until', 'after', 'over and over' and 'open-
ended' scripts. People with 'never' scripts are forbidden
to get what they really want from life. They may seek
out success in work or social life, but always sabotage
their chances of actually succeeding. People with
'always' scripts have to keep on doing the same thing,
even when they dislike it. They may, for example, take
up a particular career in order to maintain family
tradition, hate it, but feel powerless to change their
behaviour. People with 'until' scripts are never allowed
to do the things they really want to until, for example,
they have finished clearing a pending tray, planned a
forthcoming work programme, and read all the latest
professional magazines. By the time they have finished
all this, they are usually too weary to enjoy anything
else or to indulge in interests they really want to
pursue. People with an 'after' script are very different.
They can, and do, enjoy themselves, but only up to a
certain point as they believe that after, for example,
getting married, becoming a parent, retiring and so on,
disaster and disappointment are bound to strike them.
They thus live in fear of future catastrophe. People with
an 'over and over' script are condemned to keep on doing
the same thing over and over again, never learning from
mistakes. People with 'open-ended' scripts are, like

those with 'after' scripts, able to get on with life but, again, only up to a certain point, such as when their children leave home. After that, they suddenly find themselves without any interests or aims in life, and they lead purposeless, rather depressed lives thereafter.

A rather different type of sub-division has been provided by Steiner (1974), who suggests that people can receive messages which result in scripts of lovelessness, mindlessness and joylessness. People with loveless scripts receive five major destructive injunctions. These are 'don't give, ask for or accept strokes, don't reject unwanted strokes, and don't give yourself strokes'. As a result, people with this kind of scripting are unable to give or receive affection or to value themselves or others. Such people are stroke starved and they become depressed, withdrawn and isolated.

People with mindless scripts have their intuition and thinking abilities discounted by their parents. As a result, they become confused and irrational in their affective and cognitive behaviour, possibly becoming mentally ill.

People with joyless scripts are taught to repress, distort or ignore their physical and emotional needs and sensations. As a result, they may be out of touch with their physical needs, abusing themselves with excessive eating, with alcohol, cigarettes or drugs. They may also be out of contact with their feelings and be unable to make and enjoy loving relationships with others.

When parents pass messages about their wishes and expectations to their children, they also give them information about how they should respond to social and cultural norms and expectations. These are reinforced, for young children, by the educational process and other people outside the family. Thus, during the process of socialization children receive messages from a variety of sources which tell them about cultural, racial, class, family and individual expectations and norms (James and Jongeward, 1973a).

There are many ways of eliciting and discovering the script messages individuals have internalized as their life script or plan. A variety of script questionnaires have been developed (Woollams and Brown, 1979; Steiner, 1974; McCormick, 1971). Script injunctions, drivers and permissions can be drawn out in the form of a script

matrix (see Figure 6.1) and used to identify life
positions, decisions, rackets, games and life plan.

   When people discover their early script messages, and
understand the influence these continue to have on their
current behaviour, much apparently irrational and illogical
behaviour makes sense.   Such understanding can often make
an important contribution to the efforts people make in
changing behaviour about which they feel unhappy and
bewildered.

Chapter 7

Transactional analysis in use — introduction

Transactional analysis helps people to make sense of
their own and others' feelings, attitudes and behaviour.
Since it can be shared with clients, intervention is based
on a common conceptual framework and language, which
enables clients to know and understand as much about their
situation as the social workers 'assessing' or 'diagnosing'
them. The traditional 'talking and listening' style of
intervention provided by such models as task-centred,
problem solving or psycho-social casework can be integrated
with a transactional analysis framework in order to help
clients make faster and more effective progress. Role-
play, gestalt techniques, psycho-drama and other active
styles of intervention can also be used as these often
provide clients with very specific ideas about how to
solve problems as well as opportunities for testing out
new behaviours in safe surroundings.

People who use a transactional analysis framework all
share some basic assumptions about intervention, but
vary in their techniques and styles of practice. Firstly,
the user must operate from an 'I'm O K - You're O K'
position, with the overall goal of intervention being the
development of autonomy in people. Secondly, intervention
should be based on a clear contract between client and
worker about the specific goals for intervention.
Thirdly, the language and theory should be shared with
clients whenever possible, as this enables workers and
clients to operate from a shared framework in problem
solving, and enhances equality within the relationship.
Fourthly, since dysfunctional behaviour is a learned
response to unhelpful early scripting, more constructive
decisions can be made to replace early ones. Fifthly,
clients can, and should, take responsibility for their
part in the process of change, doing at least 50 per cent

of the work needed for solving problems. Finally, people
often possess the solutions to their problems, and the
social worker merely acts as a catalyst to help them
examine behaviour, work out options for change and make new
decisions.

Transactional analysis theory enables people to look at
their own behaviour within a clear and relatively simple
framework, without the worker imposing her own interpretations. Change is often achieved in a relatively short
time once people make sense of their current behaviour in
the light of early scripting and decisions. This process
of learning → understanding → change → problem resolution
is demonstrated quite clearly in some of the case material
in Chapter 9.

THE GOAL OF TRANSACTIONAL ANALYSIS

The goal of transactional analysis is to enable people to
develop their autonomy. An autonomous person responds to
current situations flexibly and realistically, rather
than using stereotyped, script-determined responses, which
are inappropriate. He takes responsibility for his own
feelings and behaviour and possesses the capacity for
awareness, spontaneity and intimacy. An aware person
knows, understands and sensitively responds to his own
physical needs and emotions, as well as to other people
and situations. A spontaneous person uses all his ego
states responsibly, flexibly and appropriately. He is
aware that his personal history shapes his current
responses, but he learns to free himself from the
unhelpful influences of the past in order to live more
fully in the present. A person with the capacity for
intimacy develops his potential as fully as possible, and
is able to make close, open and authentic relationships
with others.

The concepts relating to autonomy are based on a view
of man in which individuals are seen to strive for
emotional growth and wholeness, in spite of experiences
which restrict or impede this process. This view of man
has much in common with the philosophy of writers such
as Fromm (1957 and 1978) and Rogers (1951 and 1967) and
the humanist approach to social work found in the
writings of people such as Brandon (1976), Jordan (1979)
and Ragg (1977). Autonomy, as described within transactional analysis, may seem elusive and, like constructive
scripting, unattainable by mere humans. However, it is

suggested that, whilst everyone behaves at times in non-
autonomous ways, people can learn to develop or redevelop
their autonomy and to live out their lives from a basis
of authenticity and autonomy, rather than by using banal
or losing script behaviours.

POTENCY, PERMISSION AND PROTECTION

Social workers and counsellors who use transactional
analysis in their work with clients base their intervention
on what is known as the 'three P's' of therapy (Crossman,
1963; Steiner, 1974). These are potency, permission and
protection.

A potent worker operates from an 'I'm O K - You're
O K' position and is reliable, credible and authentic.
She is competent and professional in her approach to
practice and to the ethical conflicts inherent in social
work. She continues to develop her practice skills and
grows in terms of her own maturity and autonomy. When
people are faced with problems they need to solve, they
can find that a desire to change is hampered by
resistances which stem from unresolved early script
messages and decisions. When this occurs, social workers
need to give clients permission to make new decisions
about their feelings, attitudes and behaviour. Permissions
may be given verbally, e.g. 'It's all right for you to
take care of yourself, as well as others', or non-verbally,
e.g. a smile, touch or hug. When people are making
changes, particularly those which involve getting rid of
archaic decisions and uncomfortable, but habitual patterns
of behaviour there can be a frightening and sometimes
painful period when old patterns of behaviour are being
abandoned and new ones have not been fully integrated
into the personality. It is essential for counsellors
to recognise this situation, and to offer clients
protection throughout their struggles to change (Ford/
Hollick, 1979 - this article, although not set within a
transactional analysis context, gives an excellent example
of protection). Protection may involve extra contact,
making a 'no suicide' or 'no violence' contract, giving
a home telephone number for emergency use, involving
volunteers as extra support, building in alternative
support if a social worker is on leave, and giving plenty
of positive feedback as clients achieve their goals.

ESTABLISHING A CONTRACT

Transactional analysis practice normally involves the
establishment of an agreement or contract between a
client and a worker, in which a clear statement is made
about the problems, action needed to solve them and
hoped-for outcome. It should be specific, realistic and
achievable and stated in clear, behavioural terms, e.g.
'I have a drink problem. I drink a few pints of beer
every lunchtime and a lot more in the evenings. This is
beginning to affect my health, my marriage and my work.
I want to control my drinking, but not to stop it. I
will (a) work out a better way of spending my time and my
money, (b) enlist my wife's help, and (c) stop drinking
at lunchtime and cut down on my evening drinking.'

The contract must be agreed by both client and worker,
and related to problems the client perceives as important
to him. This can be a first step in enabling clients to
take responsibility for their own behaviour, as well as
helping them to see that they are not entirely powerless,
or helpless pawns in the hands of fate or the social
worker. The contract must be based on a realistic
appraisal of what each person can contribute to the
process of work. Client and worker must both be competent
parties to the contract. A worker should not make
contracts for problems with which she cannot work
effectively, whilst a client should not make a contract
when under the influence of drugs, or when his mental
state or behaviour precludes his full understanding of
its implications. Contracts should not violate the law,
or the values or beliefs of either a client or a worker
(James, ed., 1977; Steiner, 1974). Contracts can be
either social contracts in which the focus is on
behavioural change in relationships with others, or
autonomy contracts in which the focus is on increasing a
person's options in situations, and on developing greater
authenticity and autonomy (Holloway, in James, ed., 1977).
It is usually helpful to make a sequence of contracts,
with the early ones dealing with aspects of feelings or
behaviour which can be most readily changed. The sense
of achievement resulting from initial success can enhance
confidence in tackling more difficult problems, or more
deeply rooted pathology.

Six questions can be used to establish the degree of
client commitment to working on problems and to clarify
the content of the contract (James, ed., 1977). These
relate to the:

1 goals of intervention, e.g. 'What do you hope to
   achieve/change as a result of our discussions/work
   together?';
2 need for action to solve the problem, e.g. 'What
   do you need to do to achieve your goal?';
3 motivation and willingness to use energy in solving
   the problem, e.g. 'What are you willing to do to
   achieve your goal?';
4 roles of others. This is particularly relevant to
   social contracts when interaction with others is
   the focus of change. It deals with the ways in
   which other people can provide helpful feedback in
   relation to behaviour, e.g. 'How can your wife/
   husband/friends/other members of the group help you
   in your efforts?';
5 achievement of the goal. This deals with the way
   in which the client and others might recognise the
   behavioural changes stemming from goal achievement,
   e.g. 'How will you/others know when you have reached
   your goal?';
6 games and script-related behaviour that might be
   used to prevent achievement of the goal. This
   question often reveals, at an early stage in
   counselling, the behaviours liable to sabotage
   change, e.g. 'How might you sabotage your attempts
   to achieve your goal?'.

Ideally, a client needs to use all his ego states in
making a contract. The Adult is needed to give information
about the problem, previous attempts, if any, to solve
it, and goals sought. The Child provides energy and
motivation for solving the problem, whilst the Parent
needs to give the Child and Adult permission to abandon
old habits and to change behaviours and attitudes. It is
also important to assess whether and how a person uses
contaminated or excluded behaviour in any of his ego
states in order to maintain the problem.

With some clients it may, initially, seem impossible
to establish a clear contract. The Adult may be very
under-used or contaminated, the Free Child may be swamped
by the fears and anxieties of the Adapted Child and the
demands and exhortations of the Controlling Parent,
whilst the Nurturing Parent may be virtually non-existent.
I have found that I need to recognise clients' initial
hopelessness about their situation, and their fears about
change whilst, at the same time, sharing my belief in
their worth, their basic competence and their capacity
to change. This means confronting discounting behaviour,

giving positive feedback, and focusing on change. For
example, in our first interview, Ella seemed utterly
hopeless and apathetic, without energy or motivation for
change or any clear ideas about what she wanted from
counselling. In order to cathect Ella's Adult and to
get her actively involved in the change process, I
suggested that we have five exploratory sessions before
deciding whether we could establish a clear and workable
contract. In our early interviews, Ella reinforced her
helplessness by insisting on a lengthy account of her
history and past problems. This had already been discussed
and mulled over by Ella and her husband, as well as by
psychiatrists, on numerous occasions, but without Ella
using her exploration and discussion of her past to benefit
her in dealing with the present. It seemed important,
without under-valuing the impact of Ella's history on her
current unhappiness and confusion, to break this vicious
circle, as, by concentrating on the past to the exclusion
of the present, I continued to provide Ella with attention
for her feelings of depression, rather than for attitude
and behavioural change. I suggested that Ella write out
her history, so that our early interviews could concentrate
on the current situation. This seemed to provide the
catalyst which was needed to enable Ella to begin to use
some of her energy in her Adult. We began to explore ways
in which she had, at times in the past, been competent
and happy and as we did this, Ella began in a very slow
and tentative fashion, to use her Adult and Free Child in
constructive ways.

It is important that contracts be about real rather
than spurious change. A spurious contract would come
from Adapted Child, using phrases such as 'I'd like
to...', 'I think I might...', rather than an Adult 'I am
going to...', or 'I will...'. A spurious contract also
reinforces dysfunctional behaviour, in the guise of
changing it. For example, a person who wanted to change
a 'Hurry up' driver at work might decide to take up an
outside activity, and then use the same kind of behaviour
in that activity. Real change would be concerned with
changing the behaviour at work and would involve such
activities as delegating work, sorting out priorities,
taking a lunch break, learning to relax and switch off,
and so on. In this situation, outside activities might
be used as part of the overall strategy of change, but
not as a way of avoiding real change.

TEACHING TRANSACTIONAL ANALYSIS

Teaching transactional analysis is one of the first
steps in intervention. Although the strategies used in
the course of problem solving are not unique to transactional analysis, the use of a shared language and
framework for analysing and understanding behaviour can
provide a powerful tool for self-help and for accelerating
the process of change. However, it is important that the
teaching be given when people are receptive to it, and
not too disturbed or confused to understand it. In most
situations, initial explanations of the theory can be
given within the first one or two interviews. Once
initial emotional relief has been gained from sharing the
problems that have brought a person to a social worker,
the Adult is usually available to understand and use
information about transactional analysis.

A useful starting point is to give an explanation of
the three primary ego states. Additional information can
then be geared to the needs of the individual concerned,
although in a group setting, brief explanations of all
the major theoretical concepts may be given. Although
transactional analysis is now a complex theory, it is
quite possible to give explanations which, whilst they
may seem to over-simplify the complexity of behaviour
and personality, nevertheless provide a clear framework .
for clients to use. One of my students, when working
with an intellectually limited adolescent who took on a
parenting role within his family, likened the three
primary ego states to a bag of balloons. The client was
quickly able to understand the basic concepts and was
able to explain to the student, in Parent - Adult - Child
terms, the interaction within his family. He could see
that he used his Parent at the expense of his Child ego
state, in a family where both parents over-used their
Child ego states. As a result, he began to find ways of
using his Adult and Child more effectively, particularly
in social and work situations, where change was more
readily accepted by others.

Apart from the verbal descriptions and graphical
presentations provided by a counsellor, a client can be
encouraged to do simple exercises (James and Jongeward,
1973a, 1973b and 1975; James and Savary, 1977) in which
his personality and problems are viewed within the context
of transactional analysis. He might also be encouraged
to read one of the introductory books on transactional
analysis (Harris, 1973; James and Jongeward, 1973a). In

agencies where video is available, he might get feedback
about his behaviour in transactional analysis terms by
seeing himself on film. Transactional analysis is often
practised in a group setting and when this is the case,
clients·can often give each other feedback, using
transactional analysis language as a common conceptual
framework for understanding and explaining behaviour.

MODES OF INTERVENTION

Transactional analysis practice can be based on any of
three basic modes of intervention which are common to a
variety of therapeutic and counselling situations (Wolberg, ed.,
1967). These are the supportive, educational or reconstructive modes of intervention and counselling.

   Sometimes, a supportive, empathetic relationship, in
which support is offered during a process of problem
clarification, is sufficient. For example, Nora had
spent much of her life struggling with a weight problem
and alternating between bingeing and dieting. In a
therapy group, she was encouraged to explore the early
messages she had received about attitudes to food. It
emerged that Nora's early existence was fraught with
problems surrounding feeding. When she was born, her
mother was too ill to feed her and died shortly after-
wards. Nora's early childhood was spent between various
relatives, many of whom indulged her with rich food,
sweets, etc., in attempts to compensate her for the loss
of her mother. When Nora over-ate as a child, she did
not receive any help in setting limits on her food
intake and, as a result, she did not learn to set any
realistic controls on her eating. Nora had always thought
her obsession with and lack of control around food was
'neurotic' but once she made the connection between her
early experiences and her current behaviour, she could
see that her behaviour had once been seen by her
relatives as a helpful way for her to compensate for her
mother's death. After this, Nora became more relaxed and
less obsessional about food and diets.

   When transactional analysis is used as an educational
tool, there is a focus on helping people to change
unsatisfactory ways of relating to others and dealing
with problems. Beth was able to see that she reinforced
her 'not O K' position by redefining transactions,
discounting helpful strokes and playing Yes, But. She
learnt, during the process of counselling, to change

these behaviours in favour of complementary transactions, accepting strokes and taking responsibility for her own behaviour. These changes enabled Beth to learn to like herself, and to enjoy her work and relationships with others more completely.

When transactional analysis is used in order to change aspects of personality and behaviour, there is a focus on changing dysfunctional aspects of ego state structure and on clarifying and changing those decisions and script behaviours which are giving rise to current problems. Ella had to examine early script messages, many of which were archaic and destructive, in order to make new decisions about herself, her attitudes and her behaviour. She had to expand her use of her Free Child, Adult and Nurturing Parent and to reduce the destructive impact of her Adapted Child and Controlling Parent. Reconstructive therapy is a slow, often painful and difficult process, and it can be hampered by Child fears and Parent prejudices about change. It requires patience, creativity and not a little faith on the part of the worker.

SCHOOLS OF TRANSACTIONAL ANALYSIS

Although there is now a proliferation of theories and practices within transactional analysis, three major styles of practice can be discerned (Barnes, ed., 1977). The Classical School, founded by Berne, concentrates on the development of an uncontaminated Adult, thus enabling the Adult ego state to act as the executive of the personality, and to mediate between the needs of the Child and the demands and exhortations of the Parent ego states. The Cathexis School, founded by Jacqui Schiff, focuses on the problems arising from the lack of a functional and constructive Parent ego state. Among the strategies she has developed is her reparenting work with people who have been diagnosed as schizophrenic. In reparenting, the emphasis is on regressing people to a stage before the development of their Parent ego state and on replacing their internalized, destructive messages with new permissions and, therefore, with a new and constructive Parent ego state. The Redecision School, founded by the Gouldings, concentrates on the subjective world of the individual, and on dealing with Child ego state impasses, or blocks to change, which interfere with problem solving and the development of autonomy.

However, when transactional analysis is used in social

work and counselling an eclectic model, drawing on a range of approaches to theory and practice seems to be the most appropriate. Chapter 8 will therefore examine practice within the theoretical structure presented in Chapters 1-6, and will draw on ideas and concepts from all the schools of transactional analysis theory.

Transactional analysis in use — assessment and process

ASSESSMENT

The assessment of problems can be aided and enhanced by
exploring them within a transactional analysis framework,
and by asking questions relating to the various elements
within the theory. Some examples of these questions
might be:

1 personality structure - are there issues relating
   to ego state structure and use, e.g. contamination,
   exclusion, under-use or over-use of particular
   ego states?;
2 interaction with others - how does the person use
   his ego states in communicating with others? Does
   he redefine transactions, what kinds of transactions
   does he tend to use?;
3 time structuring - what kind of stroking and time
   structure pattern does the person have? Does he
   play games as a way of maintaining dysfunctional
   behaviour?;
4 script influences - are script messages and early
   decisions influencing current behaviour unhelpfully?
   What life position is held by the person?.

The answers to these and similar questions can be
helpful to social workers and counsellors in reaching a
clear assessment of problems, working out a focus and
structure for intervention and in identifying possible
resistances to goal achievement.

The following case study shows how a transactional
analysis framework can aid assessment (Wilson, 1979).
Meg was a seventeen-year-old single mother whose presenting
problem was depression caused, she said, by living in

overcrowded conditions with her parents. The initial
referral stated that Meg wanted help in finding
accommodation for herself, baby and boyfriend. In the
first interview, I learnt that Meg's baby had been born
three months earlier. Since then, she and her boyfriend
had not been allowed by their respective parents to
spend time alone together and Meg had been told that her
job was to care for her baby and not to go out enjoying
herself. Meg felt that she was caring for her baby
quite well, but said her mother constantly criticised her
and this resulted in more tension and quarrels between Meg
and her parents.

Whilst I agreed that Meg's depression stemmed mainly
from housing problems, it seemed to me that other factors
were reinforcing this. I felt that Meg's depression was
exacerbated by the repression of her Free Child, as she
was not being allowed any closeness or intimacy with her
boyfriend. Her Adapted Child was being over-used as she
reacted to her parents' criticism of her handling of the
baby. Her Adult was being under-valued and under-used,
partly because her parents' criticism discounted her
ability to look after her baby and partly because Meg
believed she was powerless to act in order to solve some
of her problems. Meg's Nurturing Parent was also being
discounted, both in terms of its use in looking after
her baby, and in looking after her own Child needs. As
a result of this assessment, it seemed important to help
Meg find ways of activating her Adult and strengthening
her use of Free Child and Nurturing Parent by reducing
the energy she was investing in her depressed Adapted
Child ego state. In transactional analysis terms,
intervention was based on helping Meg to change the way
she used her energy, thus, it was hoped, altering her
ego state portrait as shown in Figure 8.1.

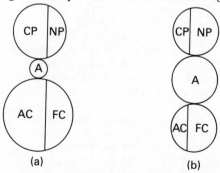

(a)   (b)

Meg at first interview   'ideal' outcome of intervention
FIGURE 8.1 Altering a person's ego state portrait

WORKING WITH EGO STATES - THE ADULT

Many problems arise from, or are exacerbated by, lack of
effective Adult functioning. As has already been shown,
the Adult can be under-used, or over-used, contaminated
or excluded. For example, a major problem in depression
and confusion stems from the inability of the person
involved to use his Adult ego state to mediate between
the Child and Parent ego states. Although intervention
may be needed in relation to all three ego states, an
essential step in problem solving is to encourage better
use of the Adult, so that it can be effective in mediating
between the other ego states and the demands of the
external world. The early stages of contact, when the
contract is agreed and clarified, and the theory relating
to transactional analysis is taught, provide an opportunity
for people to begin to use their Adult ego states more
effectively.

The use of the Adult can be further strengthened by
encouraging clients to 'stand outside' situations with
which they are having difficulty and to report back on
their reactions as objectively as possible. This can
encourage a more Adult awareness of what is happening
and it can often result in constructive ideas for change.
Sometimes writing things down can enhance the use of the
Adult. Beth used this technique very successfully, by
listing pros and cons of situations that worried her and
using her list to examine her feelings as well as her
thinking about her worries and to help her make new and
clearer decisions. She also, on occasions, wrote down
new behavioural strategies to use in situations she knew
she was going to find difficult and this enabled her to
use her Adult, rather than her Adapted Child, in such
situations. Trying out new behaviours and then reporting
back in the next interview can also enhance the use of
the Adult. Mrs Adams worked out, during one of our
interviews, specific ways for changing her behaviour
towards a neighbour whom she felt made excessive demands
on her time. She was able to succeed in this, to report
back in the next interview and then to look at ways in
which she could reinforce her new behaviours.

Berne suggests eight specific therapeutic techniques
for enhancing the appropriate and effective use of the
Adult. The first four are designed to decontaminate the
Adult, whilst the last four are designed to strengthen
the uncontaminated Adult in its role as executive of the
personality. As with other strategies, these are not

unique to transactional analysis, but their use with this
framework will be examined here. Examples are given, in
each instance, from my work with Beth. The eight
interventions consist of the following:

1 interrogate - ask questions designed to elicit
   Adult information about the problem being addressed
   (used throughout our contact to clarify problem
   areas, action needed to solve them, impasses to
   change and goal achievement);

2 specify - underline and emphasise issues which may
   need exploring at a later stage (used to emphasise
   script issues about 'being perfect' and/or 'failing'
   which needed fuller exploration during the course
   of counselling, as we dealt with some of the
   impasses to change);

3 confront - point out inconsistencies and discounting
   (used, particularly in the early stages, to help
   Beth see that she minimised her achievements by
   discounting, redefining transactions and under-
   valuing her Adult competence);

4 explain - follow up a confronting statement with
   an explanation to the Adult about the effects of
   discounting, etc. (used to give Beth information
   about how she maintained her 'not O K' position by
   redefining, etc.);

5 illustrate - use analogy, comparison or example
   to reinforce explanations and further strengthen
   the Adult (various analogies were used when Beth
   was struggling to change her 'hurry up' driver to
   help her appreciate the differences between a
   'doing' and a 'being' mode of behaviour);

6 confirm - confront a specific game, discount, etc.
   that has already been examined and dealt with, but
   been moved into another context. This often
   confirms the accuracy of the earlier hypotheses
   about games being played, driver behaviour, etc.
   It may be necessary to revert to some of the
   techniques and strategies already used in order to
   deal with this issue (used at a later stage in
   counselling, when Beth had shifted her 'not O K'
   feelings from the 'presenting problem' area of
   work to other areas, e.g. irrational fear of
   pregnancy, fears that her boyfriend would sabotage
   her progress, etc. Beth's 'be perfect' and 'don't
   succeed' script messages were, temporarily at least,
   sabotaging her chances of real change and we then
   had to deal with the underlying fears, as well as
   the presenting issue);

7 interpret - when the Adult is in the executive and
the client can make sense of interpretations,
current behaviour is explained in terms of its
links with early scripting and experiences (used,
at a later stage in counselling, to make links
between Beth's current behaviour, fears and
confusion and the script messages she had internalised
relating to 'being perfect', an impossible achievement, and 'not succeeding', an inevitable outcome
of trying to fulfil a 'be perfect' driver);
8 crystallise - summarise the situation, explore the
options for change, review progress (used, at the
end of our contact, to summarise the changes Beth
had made, examine the options she could use when
dealing with problems in the future and the
alternative supports she might use, e.g. friends,
colleagues, etc.).

WORKING WITH EGO STATES - THE CHILD

Problems can arise when the Child ego state is used
inappropriately or resists change. When the Child is
over-used, often in an irresponsible or destructive
manner, it is useful to look at ways in which a person
can meet his stimulus hunger and Free Child needs
constructively. When behaviour is socially unacceptable
or personally dysfunctional, it needs to be channelled
into constructive, but nevertheless exciting directions,
rather than merely being repressed. In their attempts
to encourage people to live more acceptably within
society's norms, social workers may sometimes discourage
creativity and risk on the part of their clients (Soyer
in McDermott, ed., 1975). Transactional analysis practice
includes the possibility of risk in undertaking and
testing out new behaviour, although this should be done
within the framework of the three P's discussed earlier.
Within social work, intermediate treatment activities,
community service project work, experiential group
experience and so on can all offer considerable potential
to clients to use their Free Child creatively. With
people who enjoy a certain amount of stimulus from having
problems, it is useful to look at new sources of stimula-
tion. When Beth was coming towards the end of our work
together, we explored different ways in which she could
get the enjoyment she obtained from self-analysis, such
as developing new counselling skills she could use in her
own work as a social worker, rather than merely using
them on herself.

When the Free Child is under-used, but there is a reasonably functional Adult, it is possible to enlist the help of the Adult in exploring ways in which Free Child creativity, enjoyment and spontaneity can be increased. This can be done by encouraging clients to identify unmet needs, to practise new, or old but discarded, ways of meeting these, and getting them to ask, when appropriate, for others to share their Free Child activities. The ways in which the Free Child can be increased are endless and vary according to the interests of the client. Beth asked her boyfriend for more touching, cuddling and physical closeness, without necessarily having to lead to full intercourse. She also started attending dancing classes and joined a woman's group in order to make new friends. Ella and her husband decided that they would share one activity together each day that they both enjoyed - cooking a special meal, watching television in front of a specially lit log fire, going for a country walk.

Resistance to behavioural change usually stems from Child conflicts, either between the various parts of the functional or structural Child or between Child needs and Parent drivers and expectations. Conflicts are often linked to early experiences and decisions and, until the client identifies the original fear and makes a new decision about his feelings and behaviour, the resistance and conflicts may continue to sabotage problem solving efforts.

Intervention focuses on two main areas. Firstly, the worker must get the client to take responsibility for his own feelings, rather than blaming others, his situation or bad luck. The worker confronts statements such as 'my wife's behaviour makes me depressed'; 'I can't help drinking too much, I'm under stress at work'; 'I had such a disturbed childhood, it's no wonder I'm a mess.' The client is asked to recognise that he chooses particular feelings or actions in response to situations, and that he must take responsibility for these. He is then encouraged to look at more effective ways of resolving problems.

Secondly, the worker must uncover resistances to change, discarding archaic messages and making new and constructive decisions (Goulding, in Sager and Kaplan, 1972). When dealing with impasses, it is usually more helpful to use techniques which enable people to focus on feelings, rather than their thoughts about situations.

Thus guided fantasy, exploring dreams, gestalt work,
role play, psycho-drama and other methods designed to
elicit Child fears and conflicts are more appropriate
than Adult discussion. Guided fantasy, for example, can
encourage a person to go back in time, reliving in the
'here and now' early experiences which have contributed
to current dysfunction. Gestalt techniques can aid a
person in acting out the warring parts of his Child, or
of his Child and Parent ego states. Role play can be
used to encourage the acting out and reliving of painful
events from the perspective of all those concerned. When
people are exploring early decisions, powerful and painful
feelings are often aroused. It is important for the
counsellor to provide support, time and caring concern
during this process. It is also important for the
feelings and decisions to be explored, not only in the
Child ego state, but also in the Adult, so that current
information can be considered, archaic messages discarded
and new decisions made. The social worker may need to
give Adult feedback and information in order to enable
the client to move forward by helping him to see that his
early decisions, whilst they were understandable in
childhood, are no longer appropriate or functional.

WORKING WITH EGO STATES - THE PARENT

A problem in some situations is that of over-use of the
Parent ego state in looking after others, and under-use
in looking after self. This can result in 'smothering'
relationships, in which the person with the Unhelpful
Nurturing Parent encourages dependency. There is usually
a direct link between a rescuing Parent and repressed
Free Child, and a change in one ego state normally
influences the other. A person who spends too much of
his time and energy looking after others often feels
resentful, righteous or angry. Work needs to be
directed towards reducing the amount of rescuing being
done to others, and to increasing internal nurturing, so
that Free Child needs are more effectively met. Again,
the Adult can usually be enlisted in working out new ways
of behaving. Tess's work with mothers and Ada's attempts
to look after her own needs rather than others (see case
material in Chapter 9) are good examples of the way in
which work directed to reducing the amount of energy in
the Parent can influence the Free Child positively.

As I have already discussed, problems sometimes stem
from the internalization of destructive and archaic

parental messages. Social workers may need to give
people permission to have, as Berne says, 'a friendly
divorce' from their parents and hence from their
influence in terms of unhelpful Parent messages. When
parents are still alive, it can be useful to check out
the accuracy of current perceptions about early experiences
(Spark, in Tolson and Reid, eds, 1981). People often discover
that the messages they have internalized are distortions
of their parents' intentions and this discovery alone
can help people to 'let go' of archaic script messages.

Although, ideally, people would always make redecisions
about early messages, getting rid of dysfunctional ones
completely, this process can be lengthy and difficult.
I have found that, once people understand the effects of
parental messages and develop some techniques for dealing
with them, they can function extremely adequately, even
though they have not eliminated the early script messages.
Beth, for example, still tends to use her Unhelpful
Controlling Parent in setting herself unrealistic goals
at work, but she is now much more aware of what she is
doing and she is able, when she begins to see this process
taking place, to rethink her goals more realistically.
She no longer gets herself into a vicious circle of
depression and anxiety.

WORK INVOLVING TWO OR MORE EGO STATES

When confusion forms part of a problem, there is usually
internal conflict between ego states. When this occurs,
it is useful to encourage people to try out exercises
designed to separate Parent attitudes and values from
Adult data and Child feelings. Listing available options,
and exploring outcome (Adult), feelings (Child) and
attitudes and opinions (Parent) can also help people to
deal constructively with confusion and their inability
to make decisions (Karpman, 1971). Drawing up egograms
or ego state portraits can also identify areas for
change (Dusay, 1977). Two- or three-chair exercises,
in which people move from one chair to another, exploring
problems from the point of view of differing perspectives
or of different ego states can often help to clarify
issues and decrease confusion.

Kate, for example, found that her tendency to get
involved in unhappy relationships with men was clarified
when she did a three-chair exercise. In the Parent chair
she found she had a prejudice that 'men couldn't be

trusted'; in the Adult chair, she knew that her current
relationship was reciprocal in its trust and affection
and the man was trustworthy; in the Child chair she had
happy Free Child feelings about the relationship, but
Adapted Child fears that 'men always let you down.' This
exercise helped Kate to see that her Parent and Adapted
Child opinions and fears stemmed from early script
messages from her mother. Whilst they might have been
correct for Kate's mother, Kate decided that they were
no longer appropriate for her and she made a decision to
trust her Free Child feelings and her Adult data.

In general, it is usually easier to concentrate on
stimulating the under-used ego state when working on
issues relating to the use of ego states (Dusay, 1977).
The ego state which is over-used may well be activated
in order to sabotage the change efforts, and work needs
to be skilfully directed to dealing with potential
sabotage, as well as to helping clients to use all their
ego states more effectively and appropriately.

WORKING ON COMMUNICATION PROBLEMS

The goal of transactional analysis, as communication
theory, is social control, or the handling of transactions
with others in flexible and appropriate ways. Since,
when people communicate with others they tend to choose
transactions which fit their frames of reference, it is
possible to form some hypotheses about which ego states,
rackets and games are favoured. Script issues and other
facets of behaviour can also often be identified from
the types of transactions used. Whilst problem solving
may need to address all these issues, particularly in
more deeply rooted pathology, it can often be sufficient
to deal with issues relating to communication problems,
as a change in patterns of interaction can often
influence other aspects of personality and behaviour in
a constructive way. The major problems in communication
stem from too inflexible a response to others, resulting
in dysfunctional crossed transactions or consistent use
of the various kinds of ulterior transactions, indicating
that games are being played. Responses may, on the other
hand, be too flexible, leading to dysfunctional complementary transactions.

A person who responds in a complementary fashion,
regardless of the situation, may need to learn to use
crossed transactions effectively. Pat was a very

competent person who normally used all her ego states
flexibly. However, one of the men for whom she worked
as a secretary consistently used Unhelpful Controlling
Parent in his transactions with her, by unfair criticism
and fault-finding. He clearly intended, and usually
succeeded, in eliciting a compliant and upset Adapted
Child response from Pat. Pat needed to learn to use
other ego states, such as Adult or Free Child, to cross
the transaction, with the intention of changing or
terminating the dysfunctional communication and handling
the situation, from her side at least, more effectively.
Beth would hear most comments as coming from Controlling
Parent, and respond from Adapted Child. She needed to
listen more accurately and to learn to use Free Child,
Adult and Parent in her responses, thus extending and
improving her range of communication.

Feedback from others, role play, assertiveness and
social skills training and the use of audio and video
recordings can all be used for clarifying problems
relating to transactions, and for practising new ways
of communicating. Feedback confronts and clarifies the
kinds of transactions and ego states being used, whilst
role play and other techniques provide an opportunity
for people to test out new ways of responding in safe,
simulated situations prior to practising them in the
world outside.

WORKING ON TIME STRUCTURING

An understanding of the way in which people meet their
psychological hunger for strokes through their time
structuring can be useful, both in identifying problem
areas, and in reinforcing the importance of replacing
dysfunctional attitudes, feelings and behaviours with
more constructive ones. For many people, problems stem
from a lack of strokes, or a failure to accept helpful
and constructive strokes they receive from others.
Exercises such as the one provided in Figure 8.2 can
help people to work out their stroke profile (McKenna,
1974). Giving feedback when people discount strokes,
reinterpret them or behave in such a way that they
encourage destructive strokes, also highlights stroking
patterns. Social workers can provide a rich source of
strokes while people work on changing behaviour. They
can also confront situations in which people discount
strokes in order to maintain a dysfunctional frame of
reference and can help people to work out what they want

		Always	Often	Sometimes	Seldom	Never
Give	Helpful					
	Unhelpful					
Receive	Helpful					
	Unhelpful					
Accept	Helpful					
	Unhelpful					
Refuse	Helpful					
	Unhelpful					
Ask for	Helpful					
	Unhelpful					

Instructions: put a ✓ in the boxes in relation to your present pattern of strokes, and a X in the boxes as you would like to be in terms of your pattern of strokes.

FIGURE 8.2   Stroke profile exercise (adapted from McKenna, J. (1974)).

to change in their stroke profile. They can explore with clients ways of changing their stroking pattern and provide support during the process of change. As with other aspects of behavioural change, there are several kinds of process involved.

For example, someone who actually receives a number of constructive strokes but who discounts, rather than accepts them, needs to practice accepting strokes, and to explore why he has chosen to discount them. Someone who receives strokes for some behaviour, such as Adult competence, but not others, such as Parent nurturing or Free Child enjoyment, might need to increase the situations in which he can use Parent and Child behaviours, or to learn to ask for the kind of strokes he needs for these ego states. Someone who is fearful of trusting others might need to learn to give/accept without fearing rejection. Someone who accepts unhelpful strokes might need to learn to reject them and to work out ways of getting and accepting helpful strokes from others. Ella, for example, said that she never received any helpful strokes, but it was clear from our interviews that she rejected and discounted the ones she did receive in order to maintain her 'not O K' life position. Part of our work together was to help Ella to hear and accept the helpful strokes she received from others.

As the way in which people structure their time often reinforces dysfunctional behaviour, an analysis of time

structuring can help them to identify where they most
need to make changes. The use of an exercise in which a
person records his time structuring over a specific
period can provide information which can act as a basis
from which plans for change can be made (Woollams and
Brown, 1979).

People who spend much of their time by withdrawing
from others might respond to a task-centred approach
designed to increase their contact with others gradually.
They could gain confidence and skill in a social skills
group or join a self-help or therapy group designed to
meet the specific needs of shy and withdrawn people.
Sometimes, people spend too little time in constructive
withdrawal and they need to increase their time alone,
in order to be in touch with inner thoughts, feelings and
needs and to recharge themselves for the demands of their
everyday lives. Learning to be a quieter, more thoughtful
member of a group, spending enjoyable time alone, doing
nothing, listening to music, meditating, yoga, relaxation
exercises and so on can all act as creative ways of
withdrawing from others.

Sometimes, people dismiss the value of rituals and
pastimes, although they can be one aspect of an authentic
style of relating to others. Such people may enjoy
intimacy of a rather claustrophobic nature with one or
two people, but miss out on the enjoyment that can be
derived from less intense, but nevertheless valuable
contact with friends, colleagues, neighbours and so on.
For others, there may be a fear of intimacy, and time may
be spent almost exclusively in superficial contact with
others which is based on rituals or pastimes. When this
occurs, people's fears about intimacy may need to be
explored, in order to help them develop richer and more
satisfactory relationships with others.

Some people may lack the stimulus and rewards that can
be derived from activities, either shared or individually
undertaken, and creative lateral thinking may be required
by workers and clients in order to help people discover
and use their abilities and potential. For others,
particularly in a culture where the work ethic is strong,
problems may arise when, for example, too much time is
spent responding to a 'work hard' message. Whilst this
may lead to success at work, such people may lead lonely
and emotionally impoverished social lives. The focus of
work may need to be on helping people to make new decisions
about their drivers and on giving them permissions to relax
and enjoy closeness with others.

Games are ulterior ways of structuring time with others, but they do provide people with strokes, although these are usually unhelpful. They also enable people to maintain their frame of reference and confirm unhelpful early messages, decisions, life positions and scripts, thus preventing intimacy.

People may attempt to engage in games during counselling interviews. When this occurs, social workers can cross transactions, thus refusing to get caught up in the game. They can expose the game by giving people Adult feedback about behaviour, and can give constructive strokes when clients are trying to elicit destructive ones. Sometimes, a counsellor may become aware of the games that people play in their relationships with partners, children, friends and colleagues. If games are being played outside the interview, social workers can encourage people to meet Free Child needs directly and to find new ways of relating to others, in which authenticity is used as a style of relating, and in which all their ego states are used flexibly and in non-ulterior ways. Whether games are being played outside or during interviews, or in both situations, it is generally more helpful to deal with them by exposing them and helping people to find constructive ways of getting their needs met.

A counsellor may need to give people permission from her Parent to encourage new decisions to be made about behaviour, Adult feedback about the way in which dysfunctional behaviour is maintained, and to use Child intuition and creativity in experiential techniques which help clients to identify their Child needs. People often try to escalate games when they find that others refuse to play them, and clients may need to make a commitment to stay in counselling during the uncomfortable process of confrontation of the games they are playing. As with other aspects of work, it is essential for the worker to give support and protection whilst people learn to break the games they are playing. Since games often occur at their most destructive in families, it is useful, wherever possible, to work with all the people involved, as attempts by one person to break games can lead to escalation and attempted sabotage by the others. When this is not possible, the person who is learning to break games may need to find ways of dealing with an escalation of games by others with whom he is in contact. Problems can often be resolved by focusing on current behaviour, but when there are resistances to change stemming from early decisions and script messages, it is sometimes necessary to deal with these by uncovering them and helping clients to make a new decision about their early unhelpful messages. Early decisions can be discovered by asking the following questions:

1   what decision has been made that is giving rise to current problems?;
2   what is being done now to maintain the early decision?;
3   what are the advantages (however dubious) of maintaining this behaviour?;
4   how is the early decision carried out in terms of behaviour?;
5   what discounting occurs in order to reinforce the early decision?;
6   what kinds of permission, information, strokes and so on are needed in order to help the person make a new decision?;
7   are there any other issues that need to be dealt with before a new decision can be made?

Script messages can be discovered by the use of a life script questionnaire and by drawing up a script matrix (see Appendix 2). Although a person may have incorporated parental messages into his Parent ego state, as well as his Child, early decisions are normally made by the Child ego state, and redecisions need therefore to be made by this ego state. Again, experiential techniques such as gestalt, sculpting, two- or three-chair work, role play and fantasy can be used to help people get in touch with early messages and decisions. The redecisions made by the Child, and perhaps by the Parent, need to be backed up and reinforced by Adult data. They also need to be lived out in the form of new behaviour. People need to work out how they will carry out their new decisions and how they will get strokes for their new behaviour, as well as looking at ways in which they might try to sabotage these changes.

Clearly, many of the techniques discussed in this chapter are to be found in other approaches to counselling, as well as overlapping with each other in transactional analysis, where the same techniques might be used to address a variety of client problems. For example, a 'talking and listening' approach might help clients to change the way they use energy in their ego states, their style of interaction with others and their early decisions. Alternatively, role play, and gestalt techniques might deal with the same issues. Whilst there is limited research evidence within transactional analysis to suggest specific approaches to particular problems, it would seem that the techniques developed by Berne and the Gouldings are more appropriately used with those emotional problems which are labelled 'neurotic' or with people who have a relatively strongly functioning Adult, whilst the approaches developed by the Schiffs are most appropriately used with clients whose difficulties are labelled 'psychotic'.

Chapter 9

Case studies in transactional analysis

In this chapter, the use of transactional analysis will be illustrated by case studies. They are by no means exhaustive, either in range of settings or styles of intervention, but they attempt to provide some cameos of how some people use transactional analysis in social work and counselling. They have been selected to illustrate the use of transactional analysis as a counselling method, its integration into other approaches to casework, its use with 'unmotivated' clients, outcome in terms of behavioural change, and client opinion about its value.

The 'how' of practice is an elusive concept and one that people find difficult to explain in detail, particularly as transactional analysis is often integrated with other models into a social worker's own personal style. As one of the contributors to the chapter said, 'It's not transactional analysis that works, but how I use it in helping my clients to get better.' Nevertheless, although these brief examples can only give a flavour of the process and outcome of transactional analysis, they are provided in the belief that they can demonstrate its value in social work and counselling.

TRANSACTIONAL ANALYSIS IN MARRIAGE GUIDANCE

Sue is a marriage guidance counsellor who uses transactional analysis as an important aspect of her work with clients. This case study looks at some of the ways in which it is used in counselling adults who have a variety of emotional and relationship problems.

Sue uses transactional analysis in two ways - firstly,

implicitly, as a diagnostic tool and, secondly, explicitly, as a shared framework in her work with clients.

'I tend always to use transactional analysis in my head...it is such a useful tool, it puts a boundary around my own chaos and within that I can get some idea of what is going on. I get the history in the first interviews and some idea of what the problem may be, and by the time I've unscrambled that in my head, I'm ready to share my thoughts with the client.'

Sue uses some transactional analysis concepts with most of her clients. If they agree to work within this framework, she gives them a short introduction to the basic concepts of ego states. After this, the process of work varies enormously, depending on the problems being presented. For example, Sue might encourage clients to draw ego state portraits of themselves and their partners.

'They get some useful surprises. The classic one is where both partners see themselves with a large Parent and the other with a large Child. Both feel they are doing all the parenting and the other is acting out the Child. Not only does this confusion about each other's roles need clarifying, but both may need to put more energy into clearly thinking in Adult. Recognition of the symbiotic collusion helps both of them to work faster.'

When clients need to develop more effective use of their Adult, Sue mainly uses listening techniques, confronting every piece of contamination and giving feedback about what she hears in order to help people to separate out Adult data from Parent opinion and Child feelings. For example, with one client who believed that he couldn't think for himself and who operated almost entirely from Child, Sue would attempt to develop his Adult by comments such as:

'That's a feeling, not a thought. Now, what do you think about it? We know how you feel, but feelings don't define reality. Feelings define feelings but not always the reality. It is legitimate for me to say "I feel you are angry with me" but not to assume that is necessarily a fact. I need to check with you whether in reality you are angry with me.'

Sue uses techniques such as gestalt, relaxation exercises, dream work, guided fantasy or written exercises in conjunction with transactional analysis, particularly

when she wants clients to get in touch with their Child
needs and wants. For example, with one couple whose
communication with each other always took place indirectly
through a third person, thus denying themselves any
opportunity for real intimacy, Sue used a gestalt technique
by literally placing herself as 'pig in the middle' in
order to highlight how they used her to avoid and block
direct communication with each other. Their task was then
to find ways of removing Sue by learning to communicate
directly with each other. With another couple, in which
the wife was thinking of leaving her husband because she
felt there was no time or space for her within the family,
Sue asked them to do a paper and pencil exercise in which
they drew out the various amounts of time they used for
themselves (my time), each other (their time) and their
children (our time). The wife, apparently unconsciously,
left out 'my time'.

'The very fact that she had left it out was an eye-
opener, and really brought home to her how little she used
her Free Child. I asked her to work out things she
enjoyed doing, both for herself and with her husband and,
once they had rediscovered some shared enjoyment and the
wife had taken some time for herself, she changed her
mind about separation.'

Sue finds concepts relating to strokes very helpful and
uses exercises, as well as discussion to help people
examine how they deal with getting and giving strokes.
She might get people to look at the ways they discount
strokes, by asking them to identify from the following
list their own particular ways of blocking strokes (Bader
and Zeig, 1976).

1   turn stroke into a put down, e.g. 'What, this old
     dress?';
2   not hear it or see it;
3   disbelieve it, e.g. 'He didn't mean it';
4   discount the other person, e.g. 'He doesn't know
     anything about ....';
5   deny it, e.g. 'That's no good';
6   neutralise it, e.g. 'It was a fluke';
7   pay for it, e.g. 'I love you' - 'I love you, too';
8   tone it down, e.g. 'It's quite nice';
9   refuse it because it's too small, e.g. 'He might
     have said something really nice';
10   exaggerate it to make it unreal, e.g. 'He said I
     was the best in the whole world'.

Sue uses a good deal of 'loving confrontation' in her
work, particularly in helping people who are stuck in
depressions linked to early experiences and scripting.

'I may ask them when they are going to decide they
have suffered enough and when they are actually going to
change, rather than talk about it.... I tell them it takes
as much energy to withdraw from life as it does to take
steps forward.   I always emphasise that point and it
always comes as an eye-opener.'

Although Sue uses a variety of other therapeutic models
and methods, she feels transactional analysis is particularly useful as an assessment and diagnostic aid and as
a framework which clients, as well as she, can use to make
sense of situations.

'It enables them very quickly to dig things out of the
unconscious, things that they are emotionally falling
over, and gives them choices about how they are going to
deal with them.   As long as people react unconsciously,
they've got no choice.   Transactional analysis helps them
to increase the options available to them and to claim
their own autonomy.'

TRANSACTIONAL ANALYSIS IN FOSTERING

Helen and her husband Tom, have been foster parents for
the past four and a half years.   This case study examines
their use of transactional analysis with two long-term
foster children, and highlights its value with adolescents
who have been damaged by their experiences before, during
and after their time in care.

When Ben, aged thirteen, arrived in the foster home,
he was described as a rather shy, retiring boy, but
Helen soon realised that he was extremely withdrawn and
that he seemed to have very little ability to care for
himself, to control his behaviour, or to make relationships
with people.   At this stage, Helen and Tom were new to
fostering, and they felt that they needed to concentrate
on building up Ben's positive image of himself, believing
it would be unhelpful if they were very critical about
his behaviour.   Helen describes her relationship with Ben
during the first two years as 'O K but not wonderful, it
was a bit like living in a black hole ... eventually I
began to feel I didn't exist.   I was giving out and giving
out and getting nothing back.   Finally, I reached explosion

point one New Year's eve when Ben came home drunk. Instead
of dealing philosophically with it, I dumped two years
resentment on him ... we'd reached disruption point because
we hadn't been honest about what was happening.'

Throughout this time, Helen had been learning about
transactional analysis and running a group in her own
home and, although she was not aware of it, Ben had
obviously gained some idea of what transactional analysis
was all about.

'The following day, Ben asked me to teach him transactional analysis and although I was aware that foster
parents didn't do that sort of thing (i.e. take on a
counselling or therapeutic role), that's exactly what I
did. Once a week, for one hour, Ben and I had a session
in which I taught him transactional analysis.'

Helen used 'T A for Teens' (Freed, 1971), which she
found immensely helpful and, at the same time, she was
given further help by the British Association for Adoption
and Fostering, who introduced her to Falberg's work on
bonding and attachment (1981) and Gessell's work on child
development (1977). This gave Tom and Helen a much
clearer understanding of Ben, as they realised that he
was stuck, in terms of his functional age, at seven, the
age at which he originally came into care. This information alone was enormously reassuring for the whole family,
as everyone suddenly realized that Ben had been expected
to behave as a sixteen-year-old, when in fact he only
had the skills and emotional maturity of a seven-year-old.
Helen felt that, since the primary Parent ego state does
not normally begin to emerge until a child is at least
six years of age, Ben's inability to care for himself
suddenly made sense.

'Once we realized that Ben did not have an autonomous
Parent ego state, we all felt ten times better. We sat
down and worked out a plan in which, basically, we helped
Ben to develop an effective Parent. We used the Schiff
material (1975) as a basis for our own thinking and took
away any responsibility we would normally expect a sixteen
year old to have.'

The whole family became involved in this parenting
process, becoming very directive with Ben. For example,
instead of expecting him to know when he needed a bath, he
would be told 'Bath now, Ben, no arguments.'

Tom, who had previously abandoned attempts to get Ben interested in sports training would, at weekends, simply knock on Ben's door and tell him, without giving him a choice, that they were going training. When the family watched the news on television, they would insist on getting opinions about events from Ben. Helen recognizes that they took risks in this approach.

'We took a lot of risks, and we made mistakes. There were times when things slipped back and we soon learnt that, as adults, we had to have total agreement about our approach and had to create an environment in which we reacted to things as they happened. We also had to take every opportunity we could to help Ben develop his Parent ego state. We told him "When you can look after yourself, we will stop this. Until you can do that, and look after others, and control your own behaviour, this is the way it will be."'

The changes in Ben, once he learnt about transactional analysis, were immediate and dramatic. Initially, he was simply relieved to have the burden of being sixteen years old removed, saying things like 'I feel so much better.' His schoolwork improved, he stopped mumbling and began to communicate far more effectively, he learnt to give and receive affection and he developed greater intimacy with other members of the family. Basically, says Helen, he grew up very quickly. He is now functioning as an average seventeen-year-old, he has a job and hobbies he enjoys and he is a happy and integrated member of his foster family. He no longer has formal sessions on transactional analysis, although he still uses the concepts to look at aspects of himself or his relationships.

With Jean, transactional analysis was used less formally, being explained and used, with her agreement, in relation to specific behavioural issues. Jean, who had been in care since she was six years old, joined the family when she was seventeen. It soon became clear that she had learnt to repress or deny her Free Child and that she had incorporated some destructive Parent messages. As a result, Jean used games and psychosomatic illnesses as indirect, dysfunctional ways of getting her needs met. The family agreed that a variety of approaches would be tried to help Jean develop her Free Child, stop playing games and get rid of archaic Parent messages.

Firstly, Jean was given permission, when she asked for

it, to be treated as a six-year-old, thus getting for
her Child, some of the loving and nurturing she had missed
out on at that age. She might choose, for example, to
sit on Helen's knee and be cuddled, or to be put to bed
and tucked up. Jean and her foster parents listed the
games she played in order to reinforce her 'not O K'
feeling about herself and looked at specific ways in which
Jean could stop playing games. For example, when she
played Kick Me, it was agreed that she would either be
confronted with what was going on by such questions as
'Do you really want a kick?' or given loving attention,
such as a hug, rather than the negative attention she
appeared to be seeking. Jean also worked out, with her
foster parents, new Parent messages which she needed to
internalize to replace the destructive ones she had
received as a small child. Jean reinforced her learning
by pinning these up on her bedroom wall. They were also
constantly reinforced by the loving, consistent affection
she received within the family.

Jean, like Ben, has changed dramatically. She says
that, without the loving concern she has found in the
foster home, and the insights she has gained from transactional analysis, she could well be dead or have an
unwanted child - two unhelpful options Jean seemed to
have incorporated into her script. Instead, she is
learning to enjoy her Free Child, and to use her Adult
and Parent in breaking up her games and in accepting new
Parent messages. Emotionally, like Ben, she has matured
and she is now able to receive as well as to give
nurturing and affection and to look after her emotional
needs in a direct, rather than an indirect way.

Whilst the use of transactional analysis has only been
one facet of the work being done to help these two
adolescents grow up, both they and their foster parents
recognise that transactional analysis has been immensely
useful in helping them to understand themselves. It has
also given them creative and useful ideas about how,
despite the disadvantages they had in terms of disturbed
and unhappy early childhoods, they can make important
emotional and behavioural changes and take responsibility
for the direction of their lives.

TRANSACTIONAL ANALYSIS IN THE PROBATION SETTING

This case study illustrates the use of a specific aspect
of transactional analysis theory as part of the casework

with a woman whose children were subject to a matrimonial supervision order.

Ann (the client) who had custody of her two children, was extremely bitter towards her ex-husband, blaming him entirely for the breakdown in their marriage, and using her energy to maintain a poor image of herself and to punish her husband by making access arrangements difficult and acrimonious, rather than to adjust to life on her own in a constructive way. After working with Ann for two years, Mary (probation officer) began to feel that 'We were saying the same things over and over again, but not getting anywhere. In order to try to change the situation I suggested to Ann that we might put aside a few sessions, in which we concentrated on helping her to look at herself through the use of life scripts.'

Mary introduced Ann very briefly to some basic trans-actional analysis concepts, and then used an informal, non-structured approach to elicit script material. She asked Ann questions based on standard script questionnaires, about the attitudes and messages she had received from her parents in relation to various aspects of her personality and behaviour. These were written down and a script matrix produced. It very quickly emerged that much of Ann's poor self-image was linked to her attitude to her mother, whom she felt she resembled. Ann had a very low opinion of her mother, but adored her father, seeing him as someone who could do no wrong. Not surprisingly perhaps, she had looked for a husband who resembled her father. When her husband found that he could not live up to Ann's expectations, he sought a relationship outside the marriage and it was this that finally led to the break-down of the relationship with Ann.

Ann began to realize that her own attitudes and behaviour might, after all, have played a part in her husband's infidelity. This discovery was a painful one, but it resulted in Ann looking more realistically at her own attitudes and at her relationship with her mother. She decided to try to improve this relationship, and as she got to know her mother's positive qualities, Ann's view of herself improved and this, in turn, affected other areas of her life.

The relationship with her ex-husband improved as Ann became less bitter towards him, access went more smoothly and the children's behaviour clearly showed that they were being less upset as the friction between their parents

decreased. The petty thieving of one of the children
stopped and both children became happier and more relaxed.
Ann also began to use her Adult ego state more effectively,
handling problems for herself for which she had previously
sought Mary's help. Perhaps the most significant change
occurred when Ann established a happier relationship with
another man. This man was much older than Ann and 'perfect'
in many ways, but at least Ann was aware of her motivation
to choose such a personality.

Six months after undertaking this work with Ann, Mary
discharged the matrimonial supervision order. Even though
Mary had continued to use her own particular counselling
style within the framework of the script work, she felt
that Ann's ability to use transactional analysis to explore
issues from the past and to change her behaviour and
attitudes were key factors in breaking the impasse that
Mary felt had developed prior to this new approach to work.

Ann was very clear that transactional analysis and the
work on her script had helped her. She felt it helped
her make sense of her unhappy feelings about her marriage,
it gave her a greater understanding of the way in which
her past relationship with her parents had affected her
marriage and this, in its turn, lifted her spirits and
resulted in a greater sense of confidence and well-being.
The process was a painful one, involving much soul-
searching, but the outcome more than compensated for the
pain in the process.

TRANSACTIONAL ANALYSIS IN A COMMUNITY HEALTH PROJECT

Tess works as a counsellor in a voluntary agency on a
community based project designed to identify potential
parenting problems at an early stage, by providing a
listening/counselling/information service to women who
are expecting their first or second child. The project
covers an estate in a northern city where housing is poor
and facilities minimal. The residents on the estate are
mainly young couples and single parent families, many of
whom are seen by the local authority as actual or
potential 'problem families'. This case study illustrates
the use of transactional analysis with clients who are
educationally, economically and socially disadvantaged.

Although transactional analysis is used in a variety
of ways, it is its use in the support groups which have
been set up by the project workers that will be examined

here. The women become known to the project when they are
asked to complete a questionnaire about various aspects
of themselves in relation to their roles as prospective
or actual parents. Different questionnaires are completed
at the ante- and post-natal stages, and if, at this stage,
problems are identified, either by the women themselves
or the workers, the offer of attendance at a support group
might be made. Some women do not need either individual
or group counselling at any stage. Some of the women
accept the offer of attending a group at the ante-natal
stage, but for others, who did not envisage the arrival
of a baby as problematic, the opportunity is not taken
until the post-natal stage.

'A lot of mothers don't realize what having a baby
would be like, and don't think they need help until after
the first flush of "woohoo, baby" has worn off, people
have stopped visiting and admiring the baby and reality
sets in.'

Each new group follows the same pattern. The first
stage involves a period during which mothers get to know
each other and discussion focuses on issues to do with
the children. When they feel safe enough, the mothers
begin to bring in issues to do with themselves or their
relationships with partners, children or other family
members. At this stage, some transactional analysis
input about ego states, strokes and transactions is given
with any further theoretical input added in relation to
particular issues the women might raise, e.g. fears about
post-natal depression, anxieties about their marriages
or worries about their handling of their children. The
women usually understand the concepts very quickly and
can see immediately the relevance for their own lives.

'One woman, when the symbiosis diagram was on the
board, jumped up, ran to the board, pointed to the Child
ego state of the mother and said "That's me, that's the
real me, that's what I've lost."'

Within the groups, the workers use a client-centred,
self-help approach. They use transactional analysis
concepts, discussion, role play, information giving and
assertiveness training to help women examine their
problems and the options available for handling them.
They avoid rescuing, and encourage women to think things
out for themselves, help them to learn to separate fact
from opinion when working on problems, and encourage them
to get the information they need in order to solve problems.

For many women, parenthood results in a sense of lost
identity and a swamping of the Child ego state, and much
of the transactional analysis input in the group and the
individual counselling which may also be offered, is
based on the concept of permissions, encouraging women to
look after their own Child needs, without losing sight of
their nurturing role with their partners and children.
One group, for example, started meeting together once a
week for a communal meal, sharing out the tasks of
shopping, cooking and child-minding. This developed into
spending the afternoon together and playing badminton,
etc. at the local community centre and, finally, into
firm and supportive friendships being made, in which
women met outside the group and, when necessary, gave
each other practical and emotional support.

Tess recognizes that it is difficult to measure the
success of preventive work, and she also realizes that
many community and social workers set up and run equally
successful groups. However, she feels that the transactional analysis input in these groups has had very real
value in helping women to enjoy their Free Child ego
states and to use their Adult ego states more effectively.
This is particularly important for women who are taking
on the parenting role and who can very easily lose sight
of all but the Parent part of their personalities. There
has been a marked increase in the confidence of many of
the women, they are more assertive, but without being
aggressive, and less isolated and friendless.

Tess realizes that transactional analysis in itself
can do little to change the quality of life for people
whose economic and social situation is disadvantaged,
but she has been heartened and excited by the way in
which the women in the project have responded to and used
it. They enjoy the humour, the simplicity and accessibility
of the language and concepts, and the way in which they can
see its relevance for their own situations. Whilst transactional analysis cannot change their economic or social
situations, it has given the women involved in the project
a framework they can use to make sense of and change at
least those relationships and situations over which they
have some measure of control.

TRANSACTIONAL ANALYSIS IN A MENTAL HEALTH SETTING

John is a psychiatric social worker who has used transactional analysis in groups for alcoholics, and when working

therapeutically with individuals who suffer from a variety
of mental health problems. This material looks at the
outcome of his group work, as well as the way in which
John is integrating transactional analysis with other
approaches to therapy.

John's group work with alcoholics was based on the
principles outlined by Berne, in which theory is taught,
specific contracts made, dysfunctional behaviour confronted,
explanations given about behaviour, and alternative ways
of dealing with situations discussed and then implemented.
John did some simple research to evaluate the effectiveness
of this form of treatment. He found that most of the group
members changed significantly in terms of their increased
use of the Adult and decreased use of Unhelpful Adapted
Child (Heyer, 1979). John thinks that this increased
ability to use the Adult ego state constructively played
a part in enabling group members to establish and maintain
sobriety. Of the twelve members of the group, six have
remained sober, three relapsed but sought further help and
then stayed sober, and three relapsed completely. For a
problem that is often resistant to therapeutic intervention,
John thinks that these results are encouraging, demonstrating
the value of a model that gives people a framework they can
use outside, as well as within, the group or the interview.

In his work with more general psychiatric problems,
John uses a variety of strategies, in which transactional
analysis is integrated with other approaches to therapy.
This case study looks at the integration with therapeutic
coaching (Baugh, 1981). Rita, the client, had various
emotional difficulties which were exacerbated by her
inability to use her Adult or Parent ego states effectively.
Coaching was used, in the first instance, to help Rita
develop effective use of her Adult. John used video to
record a session in which Rita did a two-chair exercise.
When she spoke and behaved in her normal, 'little girl'
manner, she had to do so from the Child chair. John's
interventions were designed to elicit Adult responses from
Rita. In order to achieve this, he ignored her Child
behaviour, responding to and coaching new behaviours when
she was in the Adult chair. Rita found this a difficult
session, particularly when seeing herself on the video
feedback, but despite this, there was a marked change in
her behaviour following the session. On her way back to
the hospital with John, she started behaving in her usual
'little girl' mode but suddenly began to use her Adult in
commenting on her surroundings and so on, a marked contrast
to her behaviour en route to her interview with John. Back

n the hospital, she moved into 'little girl' behaviour
n dealing with a telephone call, but when she had a
second call, she moved back into her Adult. This
demonstrated to Rita and to the hospital staff working
with her that she had an Adult ego state she could
cathect and use, and coaching was subsequently used by
ward staff when dealing with Rita's inappropriate 'little
girl' behaviour.

John feels that, whilst this approach alone did not
prove effective in dealing with Rita's obsessional
behaviour, nor fully resolve her other behavioural
problems, the combination of transactional analysis with
coaching and video all helped Rita to begin to make sense
of and to change some aspects of her dysfunctional
behaviour and to do so more quickly than with other more
conventional methods.

TRANSACTIONAL ANALYSIS IN A RESIDENTIAL SETTING

Mike is a senior probation officer who has run a transactional analysis group for the residents of a male
probation hostel. This case study looks at its impact.

Mike found that there were some difficulties in teaching
transactional analysis concepts to a group of residents
whose intelligence quotients ranged from seventy to one
hundred and forty. Nevertheless, he found that most
members of the group were able to understand and use at
least some of the concepts, particularly those relating
to ego states. They used them, however, less for making
sense of their own behaviour, and more for challenging
the behaviour of others and the 'status quo' within the
hostel.

The group members used the group, and the common
.guage that transactional analysis provided, as a forum
 telling the more disruptive members of the hostel how
.ir behaviour affected other residents. Curiously, this
.d not seem to result in an escalation of disruptive
.ehaviour. Instead, the residents who were identified in
this way seemed able to appreciate that they over-used
Unhelpful Free Child behaviour in ways that made it
difficult for them to be accepted by other people, and it
was these residents who used transactional analysis most
creatively in terms of constructive behavioural change.

Group members were also able to use Parent-Adult-Child

concepts to identify the ways in which staff often used their Parent ego states in their communication with residents. This tended to elicit Adapted Child responses and resulted in residents under-using their Adult and Parent ego states. The residents were able to use the insights gained in the group in a productive way by seeking some positive changes in the hostel regime. In a sense, transactional analysis gave them a power base from which they could challenge the authority of staff members. Even though this gave rise to some conflict within the hostel and possibly contributed to some disruptive incidents, it was generally welcomed by staff, and some desirable changes were made.

Nevertheless, despite the positive effects of the group, Mike feels that, if transactional analysis is to be used to its best advantage in residential settings, considerable thought needs to go into the planning and setting up of such groups. He would, when next running a group, attempt to get a less wide intellectual range, working with either end of the intelligence quotient scale. He would also limit the numbers in the group to about eight and would prefer that membership was on a voluntary, rather than a compulsory basis.

BEGINNING TRANSACTIONAL ANALYSIS WITH UNMOTIVATED CLIENTS

Two questions which are frequently asked by social workers who are interested in using transactional analysis with clients are, 'how do I begin?' and 'can I use it with unmotivated clients?' This case study deals with these questions by examining the outcome of the first five sessions of a transactional analysis group based in the psychiatric wing of a general hospital. The hospital psychiatrist had some knowledge of transactional analysis, and was sceptical about its value, but he agreed that a social worker, Sandra, could start a group, along with her male co-therapist. The initial referrals were of four women, all of whom were perceived as being unable to respond to traditional group therapy. They seemed over-whelmed by groups, and were non-communicative and highly defensive. Peg was extremely self-destructive. She had an unhappy home life and had frequent admissions to hospital following overdoses. Liz seemed unable to communicate with others, following a psychotic breakdown after the birth of her second child. Sara suffered from acute anxiety and she, too, had had a psychotic breakdown. Jo's behaviour was neurotic, rather than psychotic. She

was an excessively anxious, isolated person, with a
pathological jealousy of her brother's wife who, she
felt, had taken her brother away from her. Sandra says:

'We are working with women with disturbed and
unhappy lives, with disabling mental illnesses and
with little sense of their own worth. We believe that, if
we can help these women to ask for strokes directly, and
to accept new permissions to be "O K" rather than "not
O K", then we shall have contributed to their recovery.
We began very gently. We worked with the "here and now",
sharing our feelings about what was happening and
concentrating on helping group members to accept helpful
strokes and permissions as well as to value and care for
themselves.'

Peg took another overdose shortly after the group began.
She lived in a family who ignored her behaviour, but in
the group she began to share the feelings of sadness and
loss she experienced when she, in a sense, lost a day from
her life because of the overdose. For Peg, being able to
share the 'bad' aspects of herself, yet finding she was
still accepted and supported by group members, was a
totally new experience.

Liz stopped her constant rocking to and fro and smoked
less. She no longer seemed removed from the group, but
let group members know by nods and other non-verbal
gestures that she was involved in what was happening.
She even contributed on one or two occasions.

Jo discussed an incident in which she felt angry with
her brother for, as she saw it, 'letting her down'.
After expressing her anger and her determination to 'pay
him back', Jo began to look at the outcome of remaining
angry and started to explore the options for resolving
the situation. She decided to make the first move in
re-establishing friendly contact, thus moving out of
angry Adapted Child to an Adult solution.

Sara did not, in these early meetings, make any changes
in her attitudes or behaviour, but, like Peg, she seemed
to find the accepting atmosphere of the group a new and
valuable experience. Sandra says:

'So, even after five sessions, there was some small,
hesitant but hopeful change. The first success was
that all the women did in fact attend regularly, and
kept the group rule of staying in the group throughout

the session. They began, very tentatively, to share some of their anxieties and to offer support to each other.

'We use a mixture of "talking therapy" and experiential strategies, such as fantasy. We recognise that change will be slow and tentative, but we are optimistic about people's ability to change, and we share our belief in this possibility in all our interventions with group members.'

TRANSACTIONAL ANALYSIS IN A SOCIAL SERVICES SETTING

This case study illustrates the use of transactional analysis with a client who was referred to Jean, a social worker in a social services department.

Diane (client) was divorced, with an eleven-year-old daughter. At the time of her divorce she was working for a photographic firm, where she met and subsequently began to live with Jack, one of the firm's partners. When she and Jack began to live together, Diane moved to an area where she had no friends. At the same time, Jack's business partner, a woman in her fifties, became irrationally jealous of Diane, first sacking her and then making abusive telephone calls and visits to her home. Although this behaviour took place over a short period of time and two years before the referral to the social services department, Diane had been consistently depressed, weepy, anxious and tense since that time. She had not succeeded in obtaining another job and she also complained of feelings of isolation in the area in which she was living. Diane was referred for counselling in order to help her overcome her depression and anxiety.

Jean used transactional analysis in her assessment, feeling that Diane's Adult information (that the incidents about which she felt so anxious ceased two years previously and she and Jack were settled together) was being swamped by irrational Child fears of anger and depression. Diane felt she 'ought' not to feel the way she did, but she seemed unable to control her feelings, particularly her anger towards Jack's business partner, and she seemed at a loss to know how to act to resolve her problems. It also emerged that Diane had always taken on the role of 'worrier' in her own family, and it seemed likely that some of the present anxiety stemmed from her habit of worrying about things.

Jean offered Diane four sessions initially in which to
explore links between past and present worries, and to see
how Diane might begin to make some attitude and behavioural
changes. She told Diane that as long as she carried on
unfinished business from the past, her present miseries
would continue and that, if she and Diane were to work
towards a resolution of the problems, it would require
some hard work on Diane's part.

Jean did some work on Diane's script in the early
interviews, in which it became clear that Diane had
incorporated 'help other people' as a message from both
parents, 'be strong' and 'be careful' from her father and
'don't be important' and 'don't be sexy' from her mother.
Diane began to realize that much of her anxiety stemmed
from underlying insecurity about her relationship with
Jack. She also saw that she spent a good deal of her
energy looking after others' needs, but neglecting her
own.

As a result, Diane began to look at ways in which she
could be less dependent on Jack, and to recognize the
fact that her feelings were irrational, and not based in
reality. She also began to explore ways in which she
could use her Free Child more effectively.

Jean also did a two-chair exercise, in which she
encouraged Diane to express her anger about Jack's
business partner and then, metaphorically speaking, to
dump the anger in a dustbin. This was the first time
that Diane had been able to accept how much of her
depression was, in fact, repressed anger about this woman.

By the end of these four sessions, Diane felt less
depressed, and more able to take control of some of her
feelings. She had got herself a clerical job and Jack
had begun moves to leave the photographic firm where he
was still a partner. Despite these positive changes,
Diane still felt she wanted to explore her feelings and
behaviour more fully and she joined a transactional
analysis group being set up by Jean in the department.

The remainder of this case material deals with the
group and, although only Diane's part is presented in
detail, some comment is made about the process of the
group work. Jean ran the group on conventional lines,
with each member making an individual contract about
change. She says:

'In running the group, I emphasised the importance of looking at the positives in each person's life. For example, I began the group with an exercise in which group members stated two things they could do well, as well as ending with an exercise in which members had to write appreciative comments about each other. This positive reinforcement and feedback was an important part of the group dynamics. I used some theory, mainly about strokes, ego states and games. I worked on people's Adult ego states, emphasising the Adult and Child in particular - the Adult to help group members think about problems and the Child to help them use their energy more effectively in resolving issues. Most of the group members had relatively dysfunctional Parent ego states, so I did much of the Parent input.'

Although Diane's initial contracts were to (a) be more independent and (b) stop worrying about trivialities, she also expressed considerable anxiety about her relationship with her daughter. Jean used the games plan (James, J., 1973) to help Diane examine the games she and her daughter played and to help her find ways of breaking them. Diane was able to report success in this piece of work, and an improved relationship with her daughter.

Jean also used her Helpful Controlling Parent to confront Diane with the fact that she was still, despite her earlier work, holding some anger and resentment towards Jack's business partner. Diane was encouraged to explore what she had invested in holding onto this anger and she was able, as a result, to achieve a more effective 'letting go' of her angry feelings.

Diane also worked on, though did not fully resolve, her role as the 'worrier' in the family. This seemed to be linked with her problems about independence and inability to make friends. Diane realized that her worrying was a defence against sadness and disappointment, but she did not manage to identify or work through the origins of these feelings. There was, however, a more practical and, possibly, more useful outcome to Diane's work on this problem within the group setting, as she became firm friends with another group member and the two women joined a judo class together, as well as sharing other social activities.

By the end of the group meetings, Diane's depression and anxiety were greatly decreased, she was less socially isolated and her irrational anger had diminished consider-

ably. She and Jack were planning to move into a new
home they had chosen together. The case was then closed,
seven months after the initial referral, with Diane feeling
that transactional analysis had been useful as a way of
understanding and resolving problems.

CLIENT PERCEPTIONS OF TRANSACTIONAL ANALYSIS

In this final presentation, five members of a transactional
analysis group, based in a mental health day centre, give
their impressions of its value in resolving problems.
Although the five had joined the group for a variety of
reasons, they all had problems which could be loosely
classified under the heading of depression. Four of the
members were relatively new to the group and also to
transactional analysis concepts. The fifth, Val, ended
her contact with the group on the day of my interview.

It was clear that, for all five members, the value they
derived from the group was composed of a number of inter-
locking elements - the regard they felt for the therapist,
relief at finding others had similar problems, and a
feeling of being valued and accepted. Although, in
talking to me, the group members tried to separate out
the transactional analysis elements within the group, their
comments need to be set within the context of these other
contributory factors.

Val had been in transactional analysis groups for
three years, joining the present group when her previous
one ended. When she joined her first group, she was
very unhappy in many areas of her life, but felt she
could not change anything. At the time of my interview
with her, Val was a confident, competent person, clearly
happier with herself and about to start a new job in
teaching. Val had been in other types of therapy group
before her contact with transactional analysis, but she
felt they were not specific enough in the help they
provided. She says:

'With transactional analysis I felt I was getting down
to the nitty-gritty, with ideas and options about how to
change being given. I was looking for very specific
ideas, otherwise I didn't hear things, and I got these
in the group.'

At first, Val used the language and concepts of transactional analysis as a defence against change, understanding

them intellectually, but not transferring them into her
own life.

'I took an awful long time to use the ideas, and to
feel at ease with myself. I was very confused, working
on something different every week but not getting anywhere.
Finally, I realized that, inside me, I still felt that I
was stuck at the age of two and a half, and I made a
decision to use transactional analysis and the support of
the group to help me to grow up emotionally. The group
was very supportive ... for example, they gave mè a party
when I felt I was eight, as I'd not had one as a child.
It was a painful process and I often wanted to run away ...
it led to conflicts at home, but now I feel fine. I still
feel I'm a bit younger than my real age, but that's all
right. I'm enjoying being a woman, I'm more settled with
my children and, although my marriage is still unsettled,
sometimes being worse than before, sometimes it is better!'

For Val, the group provided a safe and secure setting
in which she was able to examine her unhappy feelings,
together with protection while she, in a sense, grew up,
internalizing as she did so new messages in her Parent
and her Child. Transactional analysis gave her knowledge,
which she still uses, to help her make sense of her own
feelings and her relationships with others.

Ada is a widow with a grown-up handicapped daughter.
She has spent much of her life caring for others and, in
the process, has not learnt to care for herself adequately,
at least in an emotional sense. Ada felt that her main
problem was depression stemming from loneliness, as her
daughter had started to become more independent and did
not need Ada to look after her as much. She was finding
the group helpful, not least because she discovered she
was not alone in her feelings, but also because she was
getting new permissions. She says:

'Transactional analysis has given me permission to look
after myself after all these years of looking after
others, and permission to say "no". That's something I
find very difficult, because I'm so afraid of hurting
people.'

At first Ada found the Parent-Adult-Child concepts
very difficult to understand but, as she began to make
sense of herself in relation to her early history, they
made more sense to her.

'I realize I've always been an awful worrier, often not
doing things I need to do because I get too worried to act.
Transactional analysis is helping me to get rid of my
fears and to use Free Child more. I'm beginning to
discover what I want for myself, but I am finding it hard
to change - it's very hard!'

Despite this, Ada realizes that her present unhappiness
can be changed and she is optimistic about the way in which
she can, however slowly and tentatively, begin to enjoy
herself and her life more fully.

Kay is the newest member of the group. She was still
depressed and confused, but she had, after four sessions
in the group, begun to use transactional analysis constructively. She says:

'It's helped me with my parents in particular. My
parents are very difficult, and I've often exploded about
them in the past, but knowing about, and using, the Parent-
Adult-Child concepts helped a great deal. I was able to
look at what was happening more objectively and to deal
more positively with the situation as a result.

'For myself, I'm not yet sure how I can use the ideas -
I'm still very depressed, but I believed, before I came
here, that it was impossible to change. Here, I'm
encouraged to believe I can change. I'm still not one
hundred per cent convinced, but I think the optimism is
helpful to me. It's nice to know the possibility
exists - that's important at this stage.'

Kay's comments illustrate the fact that, in spite of
a state of depression, transactional analysis concepts
can be understood and used.

Rose initially joined the group because she was
depressed about her marital relationship. Although this
fairly quickly improved, she continued in the group in
order to work on a more fundamental issue. She says:

'I've felt all my life that I was different from other
people and this makes me very isolated. I want to find
out why I'm different and I want to gain more confidence
with people. I've only just begun to understand things,
but the group is helping me to become more confident with
other people.'

Rose, like Ada, found the concepts of transactional

analysis difficult to understand, but she too has begun
to make sense of, and to use them.

'It's helped me to untangle things, and to make sense
of them. I used to think about things a lot, but they
didn't make sense to me and I'd go round in circles. Now
I've begun to sort them out. Another thing that's been
helpful is that the group has helped me to be less
secretive. I never used to like saying or showing what
I felt, and I've been helped a good deal with that.'

Although Rose did not talk about her situation in terms
of injunctions, the group seems to be helping her to
give up 'don't think' and 'don't show your feelings'
messages and to be giving her new permissions to think
and to solve problems.

Paula's main problem, when she joined the group, was
that no one would believe her or understand her. She
had a long history of establishing symbiotic relationships with others, in which they used Unhelpful Controlling
Parent, whilst Paula responded from Adapted Child,
discounting other parts of her personality. For Paula:

'The group is the safest place I've ever been in, it's
my priority at present. I've got a lot to sort out and
a long way to go, but I've discovered that I've got an
Adult I can use ... before I used to imagine that I
couldn't think straight. The group is helping me to
really use my Adult. I've also got a lot of Adapted Child
and I tend to collect around me people who put me down.
I want to learn how to use my Free Child and how to stop
getting into these situations where I use Adapted Child
so much. I'm at last getting some permission to use Free
Child and Adult and that's important to me.'

Like the other group members, Paula realizes that she
has a lot of hard work to do if she is going to change
as she would like to do, but she too, feels that transactional analysis, combined with the support of the
therapist and the group members, provide her with a framework for making these changes.

Chapter 10

Transactional analysis in social work and counselling — conclusions

Although transactional analysis is more usually classified
as one of the new psychotherapies, I have tried, throughout this book, to explore ways in which it can be
transferred into, and used within, social work and
counselling settings. In this final chapter, I will be
summarizing its value, evaluating research, and exploring
the links between transactional analysis and other models
of social work and counselling practice. Before doing
this, I will attempt to set it within its psychoanalytic
context.

TRANSACTIONAL ANALYSIS AND PSYCHOANALYSIS

Transactional analysis has been influenced by a number
of psychoanalytic theories, e.g. those of Jung and Adler,
with the ideas of Freud having had the greatest impact.
Because casework has also been influenced by psychoanalytic concepts, a frequent question from social workers
new to transactional analysis is 'how does it compare
with Freudian theory?' For many people, it is the 'poor
man's psychoanalysis', and the Parent, Adult and Child
ego states are seen merely as simpler versions of the
super-ego, ego and id.

Looked at superficially, these views seem valid. The
super-ego, or conscience, has much in common with that
part of the Parent ego state concerned with opinions,
values and attitudes. The Parent can be a harsh and
controlling part of the personality, but it also contains
a nurturing element not found in the super-ego. The ego,
or reality principle, has much in common with the Adult,
although the integrated Adult, with its ethos and pathos
aspects, is a richer, more holistic concept. The id's

instinctual nature, its concern for pleasure and gratification, seems to be similar to the Free Child, C_c and A_c elements within the Child, whilst Adapted Child and P_c behaviours which act to repress Free Child seem more closely linked with the super-ego.

However, the id, ego and super-ego are regarded as hypothetical constructs, used to explain internal influences, whereas the three primary ego states of Parent, Adult and Child are 'social realities', that is, they are behaviourally observable and linked to a person's earlier experiences. Another difference is that, for Freud, the notion of the unconscious was central to his theory, whereas for Berne, it is not considered, except in terms of writing about a preconscious life-plan in relation to script theory. A third difference concerns the relationship between the various parts of the personality. Psychoanalytic theory assumes the super-ego and id to be in conflict, with the ego as mediator, whereas transactional analysis theory suggests that the Parent, Adult and Child can be in harmony with each other.

In terms of its philosophy, transactional analysis seems to face in opposing directions. On the one hand, there is a determinist flavour, 'in which human life is mainly a process of filling in time until the arrival of death, or Santa Claus, with very little choice, if any, of what kind of business one is going to transact during the long wait' (Berne, 1967). On the other hand, there is optimism, a belief in change and the possibility of autonomy which has much more in common, as I suggested earlier, with a humanistic approach to the understanding of man.

TRANSACTIONAL ANALYSIS - LINKS WITH OTHER MODELS

When transactional analysis is compared with the various theoretical models that underpin social work and counselling links can, I think, be made with four broad categories of practice. These are where:

(a) clear behavioural criteria are established in terms of a baseline and outcome, e.g. task-centred and behaviourist approaches;

(b) work examines the way in which a person's history influences and illuminates current problems, e.g. psycho-social and functional casework;

(c) the client-worker relationship is seen as the

medium through which change occurs, e.g. Butrym's
'ministration-in-love' model and client-centred
therapy;
(d)   the focus is on the process and outcome of interaction between people, e.g. various approaches to
marital and family therapy.

(Although there is an extensive literature for all
these models, useful summaries appear in Butrym (1976),
Roberts and Nee, eds (1970), Sutton (1979 and Walrond-
Skinner, ed. (1979)).

When the links between these models are made it can
be seen that transactional analysis has, as it were, a
finger in each pie and its value as a holistic approach
to intervention becomes very apparent.

The focus in task-centred and behaviourist models on
establishing a contract, specifying problem behaviour
and desired outcome in clear behavioural terms, and on
tasks to be undertaken between interviews, has clear links
with transactional analysis concepts relating to contracts,
clearly defined goals and 'homework' between sessions.

The focus in the psycho-social and similar models on
making sense of the present in terms of a person's history
has much in common with script theory, with its concern
for discovering the early messages that influence current
behaviour. Pyscho-social approaches are also concerned to
understand and work with blocks to change, and this has
obvious links with redecision theory, in which Child
impasses to change are explored and challenged.

The 'ministration-in-love' model brings together various
approaches which can be broadly categorized as relationship-
or client-centred and in which there is an emphasis on the
client-worker relationship as the prime force for change
and 'healing'. The concern in transactional analysis that
practitioners be people who possess characteristics of
autonomy and who operate from an 'I'm O K - You're O K'
position seems to suggest, implicitly at least, that
considerable value is placed on the quality of the client-
worker relationship as an important part of the process
of change. The view, within client-centred therapy, that
people can be self-actualizing clearly has much in common
with the belief in people's ability to become autonomous,
which is integral to transactional analysis theory.

Models in which interaction is a prime focus are all

concerned to explore and understand dysfunctional
communication, as well as the roles that people take, and
the expectations they have of others, particularly in
marital and family relationships. Transactional analysis
concepts relating to communication, particularly of an
ulterior nature, rackets and games have much in common
with the explanations that underpin various interactionist
approaches.

One dimension, in social work in particular, which
seems to be lacking in the way transactional analysis is
conceptualized, is a concern with the impact of social
and economic factors on client problems. This concern is
expressed in unitary, systems and radical theories (Bailey
and Brake, eds, 1975; Goldstein, 1973; Pincus and Minahan,
1973). Social workers are encouraged to engage in work
in which they are agents of change as well as agents of
care and control. Although there is a 'radical fringe'
in transactional analysis, the way in which the concepts
relating to autonomy, intimacy and meeting needs are
usually presented, tends to encourage a preoccupation with
self (Baute, 1979). As I have suggested earlier, for
people whose problems stem from under-use of their Free
Child and Nurturing Parent, preoccupation with self is a
very necessary step in the process of enabling them to
recognize and meet their needs in a direct and authentic
manner. Nevertheless, there is a case to be made for
better integration, within transactional analysis, of
personal awareness with a wider social concern.

EVALUATION OF TRANSACTIONAL ANALYSIS

There is, within the literature, a considerable emphasis
on research (see, for example, the Transactional Analysis
Journals (1975), vol.5, no.3, and (1981), vol.11, no.3).
Unfortunately, it seldom deals with those types of
clients and problems with whom social workers frequently
come into contact. For example, a survey by Wilson (1981)
showed that, out of one hundred and twenty-four dissertations, effectiveness, with thirty-eight, was the most
popular topic for research. A closer scrutiny revealed
that only five of these thirty-eight had any obvious
links with social work practice. Another survey by
Baute (1980) showed that, out of a hundred articles
published in 1979, only twenty-six dealt with treatment,
whilst the rest were concerned with assessment, philosophy
and special applications, e.g. use in industry. The
research into the use of transactional analysis in social

work settings falls into two main groups - firstly,
studies looking at how transactional analysis is used,
secondly, studies evaluating the outcome of intervention.

Studies which deal with the 'how' of intervention
provide a valuable insight into work with a range of
client problems, e.g. drug users (Cheah and Barling, in
James, ed., 1977; Hale et al., 1974), the elderly (Baum-
Baicher, 1979; Fielding in James, ed., 1977; Spence, 1974),
the blind (Thomson, 1974, Thomson and Mosner, 1975), juvenile
delinquents (Abu-Saba, 1975; Roth, 1977), marital therapy
(Lester, 1980; O'Connor, 1977), and family therapy (Bader,
1980; Gellert and Wilson, 1978; James, J. in James, ed.,
1977).

The results of some of these studies are dramatic. An
outstanding example is the work done by the Schiffs in
treating schizophrenics many of whom were considered, by
other professionals, to be incurable. In 1965, the
Schiffs took two young schizophrenics into their home in
order to reparent them. Four years later, they had
successfully reparented fourteen young people, all of
whom were leading successful lives in the outside world
(Schiff, 1969). Although reparenting is a skilled and
difficult process, normally requiring a residential
therapeutic setting, some practitioners take on parenting
contracts with clients, in which they use some of the
concepts and techniques developed by the Schiffs (see,
for example, Reddy in Proctor, 1978, as well as the
fostering case in Chapter 9 of this book).

Many of the other studies are less dramatic in terms
of outcome, but still report enthusiastically on the
efficacy of transactional analysis. These evaluations
are usually based on the subjective views of the workers,
rather than measurable changes in attitudes and behaviour.
Those studies which focus on outcome, as well as process,
tend, in general, to be more rigorous in their methods
of evaluation and the claims made for the efficacy of
this approach are, in these instances, somewhat more
moderate. Nevertheless, these claims need to be set
against the fact that such studies have often been
undertaken with clients whose problems have proved
resistant to more traditional types of intervention. In
general, they seem to indicate some fairly positive
results with very difficult problems and extremely damaged
people.

For example, Justice and Justice (1977 and 1978) reported

that, out of thirty couples whose children had been taken into care following parental abuse, twenty-two completed a transactional analysis group successfully, i.e. with significant attitude and behavioural change. This resulted in the children being returned and, at the time of the study, there had been no further reported incidents of abuse.

Adams (1974), in a study of recidivists, showed that seventeen out of twenty prisoners gained some control over their destructive behaviour. The men reported an increase in authentic feelings and positive regard towards themselves and others, they committed fewer breaches of prison regulations and the reports evaluating their attitudes, work record and behaviour also indicated that there had been considerable improvements in all these areas.

Studies of the efficacy of intervention with delinquent adolescents (Garber et al., 1976; Jesness et al., 1972 and Jesness, 1975) showed similarly positive results. The subjects in these studies were tested for a wide variety of attitude and behavioural changes which can be summed up in terms of increased self-worth and behavioural control. Nevertheless, a cautionary note needs adding. Jesness's study was a comparative one, contrasting and comparing transactional analysis with behaviour modification. He found that transactional analysis was, of the two approaches, only slightly more effective. This is in contrast with Smith and Glass (Clare with Thompson, 1981) who compared a range of new psychotherapies in terms of outcome in a variety of problems and found that behaviour modification was slightly more effective than transactional analysis!

There is a tendency in some of the more proselytizing literature to see transactional analysis as a speedy cure for almost any problem. Studies in which intervention occurred over a relatively short time span would seem to indicate that its impact was either non-existent or slightly negative (Arnold, 1975; Clayton and Dunbar, 1977). Whilst it would appear that people can gain a cognitive understanding of the theory quite quickly, such an understanding does not, in itself, lead to behavioural change. It seems that for many problems transactional analysis needs to be used consistently and over a consider- able period of time if people are to move from cognitive understanding to integration, use and behavioural change.

It is perhaps difficult to draw too many firm conclusions from these research studies, and I concur with Baute's

(1980) plea for more research. Yet even with this limited research evidence, it would still seem reasonable to suggest that transactional analysis appears to be a very effective approach to a variety of behavioural and relationship problems.

CONCLUSION

Mention has already been made of the way in which the presentations of transactional analysis can tend to alienate people, and lead to a confused, rather than a clear, understanding of the concepts. It is also discussed, on occasions, as if it were a creed for living rather than a framework, albeit a useful one, for understanding behaviour (Clare with Thompson, 1981; Kovel, 1978). One danger for any new theory, and transactional analysis is no exception, is that its adherents see it as the only correct or genuine theory (Furlong, 1977). It is essential to see transactional analysis as one model of human behaviour and to recognize that 'any model ... is partial humbug: only a map, and as such a very incomplete representation of reality' (Baute, 1979). Although this approach has considerable potential for helping unhappy people to understand and resolve their problems, the limitations of the theory, as well as the complexities and paradoxes within human nature warrant, perhaps, a fuller study than they seem, so far, to have received (Charny, 1974).

For those social workers who see this approach as a useful additional tool, there can on occasions be problems in translating cognitive understanding into effective use. It is desirable, whenever possible, for people to have opportunities for further training, supervision and support, if they are to use transactional analysis effectively and competently.

Transactional analysis can be used with a variety of clients, including those who are poorly motivated or resistant to other forms of intervention. It is important to recognize that, particularly when people are new to using this approach, success is likely to be greater with those clients who are genuinely concerned to understand and change their behaviour. Transactional analysis is not an easy option and it does require a high level of understanding, skill and commitment from those social workers and counsellors who use it. In spite of these limitations in the use of transactional analysis, they are, to my mind, far outweighed by the advantages.

Firstly, transactional analysis is a self-help approach, which demystifies therapy and brings complex ideas within reach of the majority of people. It thus gives them a framework they can use to make sense of their own and others' behaviour, as well as a range of ideas about how they can make effective and lasting behavioural changes. Secondly, it is non-threatening, as it concentrates primarily on observable behaviour, on giving people feedback about how they are maintaining problems and on what they can do to change. Thirdly, it can be used with a wide range of people and problems, including those who are emotionally healthy as well as those who are emotionally or mentally disturbed. Fourthly, research evidence, though still relatively sparse, does suggest that it seems to be faster and more effective in resolving problems than some of the more traditional therapies (James, ed., 1977). A final, but perhaps major, advantage is that social workers and counsellors can use transactional analysis as a framework to make sense of their own as well as their clients' behaviour, and to experience for themselves its value and effectiveness.

Although the tasks undertaken by social workers and counsellors are many and varied, often being concerned as much with service delivery and administration as with counselling, the views of the Barclay Committee report (1982) are worth noting:

It is essential that social workers continue to provide counselling ... we use the word to cover a range of activities in which an attempt is made to understand the meaning of some event or state to an individual, family or group and to plan, with the person or people concerned, how to manage the emotional and practical realities which face them.

If the value of counselling as an integral part of the 'helping professions' activities is accepted, transactional analysis offers, I would suggest, a useful, effective, credible and exciting contribution.

Appendix I

Information about the British Institute of Transactional
Analysis can be obtained from (at the time of going to
press):

ITA,
Box 4104,
London, WC1 N3XX.

There are various kinds of membership and fees for
the ITA, depending on whether or not the member is
undergoing any formal training in transactional analysis.

The ITA publishes three newsletters annually. These
give details of training workshops, study and therapy
groups throughout the country. A journal is also
published annually, containing articles on transactional
analysis theory and practice.

Although the ITA (in conjunction with the European
Association for Transactional Analysis) is currently
considering setting up its own training and certification,
at present (1982) anyone wishing to undertake formal
training has to do so under the aegis of the American
International Transactional Analysis Association, which
sets standards for training and practice. However,
anyone wishing to consider training can normally find
teaching members qualified to supervise new trainees,
within his or her own country. A prerequisite of undertaking training is membership of the ITAA, whose address
is:

ITAA,
1772, Vallejo Street,
San Francisco,
California, 94123, USA.

There are, as with the ITA, various categories of membership and differing fees.

REGULAR MEMBERSHIP

This requires the member to have undertaken a short training course run by a provisional teaching or teaching member of the ITAA (these courses are normally referred to as '101' courses). Many people begin to develop their understanding and use of transactional analysis through attending such introductory courses, as well as through training workshops and therapy groups.

ADVANCED MEMBERSHIP - CLINICAL

A clinical member of the ITAA is qualified to practice transactional analysis for the purposes of therapy. Training is spread over two or three years and is on a part-time basis. Trainees are required to undertake an agreed minimum number of hours as a practitioner, using transactional analysis with individuals, couples, families or groups. This practice is supervised by a training member. Trainees are also expected to attend advanced training workshops, to make presentations at these and to complete a written and oral examination. Most trainers also expect their trainees to spend some part of their training in therapy themselves, as a high degree of personal integrity and maturity is regarded as an essential prerequisite for competent practice.

ADVANCED MEMBERSHIP - SPECIAL FIELDS

Special fields members undertake training in educational, counselling, or management use of transactional analysis. Although each training contract is individually negotiated and the supervision connected with the trainees' special field, the other requirements will be similar to those of clinical trainees, although there may be less emphasis on personal development through therapy.

Appendix 2 A script questionnaire

People vary in the way in which they undertake script work with clients. Some simply translate the information given about a client's background into a script matrix (see Figure Appendix 2.1); others use a script questionnaire.

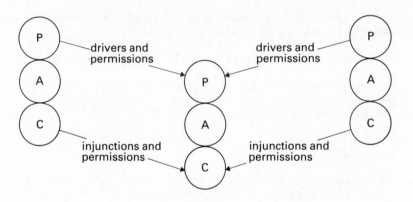

Parental injunction (message from parents' Child – restrictive) 'Don't ....'
Parental permission (message from parents' Child – constructive) can be 'Do ...' or 'Don't ...'
Parental driver (message from parents' Parent – restrictive) 'Do ...'
Parental permission (message from parents' Parent – constructive) can be 'Do...' or 'Don't...'
Basic Life position
Racket feeling
Favourite games
Decision

FIGURE APPENDIX 2.1 Script matrix (adapted from McCormick, 1971)

Although there are now a number of variations (Berne, 1972; Holloway, 1973; McCormick, 1971; Steiner, 1974; Woollams and Brown, 1979), they have much in common. The questionnaire below is adapted from Holloway (1973). When using a questionnaire, it is useful to get brief and succinct replies to the questions.

Question 1 can provide information about life positions and decisions.

Questions 2 - 24 can provide information about parental messages relating to the person's injunctions, drivers and permissions, as well as showing how parents may have modelled feelings, attitudes and behaviours to their children.

Questions 25 - 32 can provide information about the elements of the person's script, e.g. decisions, rackets, games, discounting, life position.

Questions 33 - 41 focus on possible script outcomes, particularly for people with loser scripts.

Questions 42 - 45 focus on racket feelings.

Questions 46 - 56 focus on areas for change and possible sabotage. They can be used to help in the establishment of a contract.

LIFE SCRIPT QUESTIONNAIRE

1   what kind of person are you?
2   what kind of person was your mother?
3   what kind of person was your father?
4   did any other adults live in your home before you were ten years old? (If yes, briefly describe each one.)
5   what was your mother's favourite saying about life?
6   how did your mother praise you - what did she say?
7   how did your mother criticize you - what did she say?
8   did your mother usually show her feelings in a particular way?
9   what did you do to help your mother when things went wrong?
10 what was her advice to you when you were a child?
11 what was your father's favourite saying about life?

12   how did your father praise you - what did he say?
13   how did your father criticize you - what did he say?
14   did your father usually show his feelings in a
     particular way?
15   what did you do to help your father when things
     went wrong?
16   what was his advice to you when you were a child?
17   when you were punished, what was mild and what was
     severe?
18   which punishment was most common?
19   what nicknames have you had? What did they mean?
20   briefly describe how grown-ups talked to you as
     a child;
21   what did your mother hope you would be?
22   what did your father hope you would be?
23   are you closer to what your mother or your father
     wanted?
24   what feelings, thoughts or attitudes were you not
     to reveal in your childhood?
25   what do you say and believe about life now?
26   what did you say and believe about life when you
     were a teenager?
27   what did you say and believe about life when you
     were at school?
28   what did you say and believe about life before
     you started school?
29   what do you most like about yourself?
30   what do you most dislike about yourself?
31   what childhood stories did you like best?
32   what person in the stories did you like best and
     what did you like about the person?
33   have you ever thought that you were mentally ill,
     or that such a thing might happen?
34   if someone disagrees with you, do you generally
     argue or give in?
35   do you believe you are getting nowhere or that
     your life has no purpose?
36   have you ever thought of suicide?
37   have you ever wished that someone else would die?
38   suppose your present life continues, what will
     you be in another five years?
39   at what age have you thought you might die and how
     would it occur?
40   how would you like people to remember you when you
     are dead?
41   how might others remember you when you are dead?
42   what physical symptoms do you frequently have?
43   when things go wrong, describe the feeling you
     most often have;

44 how early in your life do you remember such
    feelings?
45 describe the circumstances most often related
    to those feelings;
46 how do you wish your mother might have been
    different?
47 how do you wish your father might have been
    different?
48 if you were given wishes, what or how would you
    change yourself?
49 what do you most want in life?
50 what do you expect from me?
51 have you had social work or counselling help before?
    (If yes, give details.)
52 how did you benefit?
53 how were you dissatisfied?
54 what do you hope will be done in the process of
    the change you now seek?
55 how will you and I know that you have got what you
    came for?
56 when you change as you want to, what other troubles
    do you believe you might have?

Glossary of the main transactional analysis terms used in text

Activity - a way of structuring time by dealing with the demands of the external world, e.g. work, cooking.

Adapted Child - see Child.

Adult - one of the three primary ego states, characterised by thinking and the ability to process information and make decisions.

Autonomy - the condition of dealing with situations flexibly and realistically, instead of using stereotyped, script-determined responses. An autonomous person possesses the capacity for awareness, spontaneity and intimacy.

Behavioural Diagnosis - see Diagnosis of Ego States.

Cathexis - the flow of psychic energy between ego states.

Cathexis School - the school of transactional analysis founded by Jacqui Schiff, in which the focus is on reparenting, i.e. replacing dysfunctional ego states with functional ones.

Child - one of the three primary ego states, characterised by emotional responses to situations, as well as creativity, spontaneity, intuitive thinking and early, learned behaviours.

   Child, Adapted - a sub-division of the primary Child ego state. A second order, functional ego state,

141

characterised by a variety of affective and behavioural adaptations to the expectations and demands of the external world.

Child, Free - a sub-division of the primary Child ego state. A second order, functional ego state, characterised by a variety of spontaneous, creative and impulsive feelings and behaviours.

Classical School - a school of transactional analysis, founded by Eric Berne, in which the emphasis is on the development of an uncontaminated Adult.

Complementary Transaction - see Transaction.

Constancy Hypothesis - the hypothesis that the amount of psychic energy within a person remains constant, although it can flow and become redistributed between ego states.

Contamination - the condition in which ego states fail to operate as discrete entities.

Controlling Parent - see Parent.

Crossed Transaction - see Transaction.

Decision - made by a child in response to messages from parents and others, and determining his life position and script.

Diagnosis of Ego States - the identification of ego states being used in internal transactions or transactions between people.

- (a) Behavioural - achieved by analysing words used, gestures, tone of voice, etc.

- (b) Historical - in which current feelings and behaviours are linked to past experiences.

- (c) Phenomenological - in which a person re-experiences feelings from early childhood when faced with a similar experience.

- (d) Social - achieved by analysing the interactions between people, and observing the influence that one person is liable to have on the other involved in the transaction.

Discounting - the denial or ignoring of the existence or significance of a problem, the possibilities of change or of the abilities a person has available for resolving the problem.

Drama Triangle - a model of games (q.v.) in which two people move between the different roles of:

(a) Persecutor - the position of being over-critical, authoritarian, and controlling.

(b) Rescuer - the position of appearing to help others, but of actually encouraging dependency.

(c) Victim - the position of feeling unjustly treated and of blaming others for one's problems.

Driver - an unhelpful message sent from the Parent ego state of parents and others, and received by the Parent ego state of a child, usually stated in the form of 'do....'

Egogram and Ego State Portrait - a visual representation of energy distribution between ego states.

Ego State - a system of thoughts and feelings which motivates a related set of behaviour patterns.

Exclusion - the condition in which a person uses only one or two of his ego states, to the exclusion of the rest.

Executive - the cathected ego state, into which psychic energy has flowed.

First Order Analysis - classification and description of the three primary ego states, i.e. Parent, Adult and Child.

Frame of Reference - an affective, cognitive and behavioural 'set' used by a person in relation to himself, others and the environment.

Free Child - see Child.

Functional Analysis - see Second Order Analysis.

Game - a way of structuring time, in which people use ulterior transactions (q.v.) in order to maintain a dysfunctional frame of reference, unhelpful decisions, life positions and scripts.

Game Plan - a method of identifying the games that people play and for discovering ways of breaking them.

Historical Diagnosis - see Diagnosis of Ego States.

Injunction - an unhelpful message sent from the Child ego state of parents and others, and received by the Child ego state of a child, usually stated in the form of 'don't....'

Intimacy - a way of structuring time, characterised by openness, authenticity and honesty.

Lax Boundary - the condition in which energy moves too freely between ego states.

Lesion - the condition in which a 'sore spot' occurs within an ego state.

Life Position - the general attitude a person has towards himself and others, determined by a person's early experiences and decisions.

Message - a verbal or non-verbal communication passed to a child from his parents and others and which he internalizes to form the basis of his script.

Nurturing Parent - see Parent.

Parent - one of the three primary ego states, characterised by attitudes, values, opinions and taught concepts, as well as the ability to look after oneself and others.

> Parent, Controlling - a sub-division of the primary Parent ego state. A second order functional ego state, characterised by controlling, judgmental, critical behaviours, in which various kinds of limits are set on self and others.

> Parent, Nurturing - a sub-division of the primary Parent ego state. A second order, functional ego state, characterised by nurturing and parenting behaviours towards self and others.

Pastime - a way of structuring time, consisting of conversations about safe topics, in which a degree of consensus can be expected.

Permission - a constructive message which a child receives from parents and others, and which encourages the development of autonomy and the capacity for intimacy.

Persecutor - see Drama Triangle.

Phenomenological Diagnosis - see Diagnosis of Ego States.

Racket - the process by which a person manipulates others in order to confirm and reinforce his early decisions, life position and script.

Redecision School - a school of transactional analysis, founded by the Gouldings, in which the focus is on removing Child impasses to change.

Rescuer - see Drama Triangle.

Rituals - a way of structuring time, consisting of predictable, stereotyped transactions about which there are known and widely accepted conventions.

Script - the totality of messages internalized by a child, his decisions about these, and his life position. Together these form the basis for a person's script.

Second Order Analysis - the breakdown of the three primary ego states into smaller components, or ego states within ego states.

   Second order functional analysis - classifies these in terms of their behavioural or functional components.

   Second order structural analysis - classifies these in terms of their content or structural component.

Social Diagnosis - see Diagnosis of Ego States.

Stroke - a unit of recognition, either verbal or non-verbal, providing stimulus and recognition for a person.

Structural Analysis - the description and classification of the various ego states, first and second order, that make up personality - see also Second Order Analysis.

Symbiosis - the condition in which two people, neither of whom utilises a full range of ego states, together behave as one person.

Time Structuring - the ways in which people structure their time in order to obtain the strokes they need, to reinforce their early decisions and life positions and to further their script.

Transaction - a verbal or non-verbal stimulus and its
response, passing along paths or vectors between the
internal ego states of an individual, or between the ego
states of a sender and a respondent.

Transaction, Complementary - one which occurs between
two people, involving one ego state in each and with
the vectors therefore parallel.

Transaction, Crossed - one which occurs between two
people, involving three or four ego states in all,
and where vectors usually, but not always, actually
cross.

Transaction, Ulterior - one which occurs between two
people, consisting of two levels of message, one
verbal and one non-verbal, which are not congruent.
It involves three or four ego states in all. Ulterior
transactions can be further divided into angular,
duplex, gallows, blocking or tangential transactions.

Transactional Analysis

(a)   the theory of personality in its totality.

(b)   the analysis of transactions that occur between
people.

Ulterior Transaction - see Transaction.

Victim - see Drama Triangle.

Withdrawal - a way of structuring time, in which a
person withdraws, mentally and/or physically from others.

References

ABU-SABA, M. (1975), The female juvenile delinquent, 'Transactional Analysis Journal', vol.5, no.1, pp.62-5.
ADAMS, L.W. (1974), Use of transactional analysis with adult male prisoners, 'Transactional Analysis Journal', vol.4, no.1, pp.18-19.
ARNOLD, T.J. and SIMPSON, R.L. (1975), The effects of a transactional analysis group on emotionally disturbed school-age boys, 'Transactional Analysis Journal', vol.5, no.3, pp.238-40.
BADER, E. (1980), A cured family has problems, 'Transactional Analysis Journal', vol.10, no.2, pp.143-6.
BADER, E. and ZEIG, J.K. (1976), Fifty-seven discounts, 'Transactional Analysis Journal', vol.6, no.2, pp.133-4.
BAILEY, R. and BRAKE, M. (eds) (1975), 'Radical Social Work', London, Arnold.
BARCLAY, P.M. (1982), 'Social Workers - their Roles and Tasks', London, National Institute for Social Work.
BARNES, G. (ed) (1977), 'Transactional Analysis after Eric Berne', New York, Harper & Row.
BAUGH, J.R. (1981), Therapeutic coaching, 'Transactional Analysis Journal', vol.11, no.4, pp.300-3.
BAUM-BAICHER, C. (1979), Age is in the eye of the beholder : a multi-level treatment approach for depressed elderly clients, 'Transactional Analysis Journal', vol.9, no.4, pp.261-4.
BAUTE, P.B. (1979), Intimacy and autonomy is not enough, 'Transactional Analysis Journal', vol.9, no.3, pp.170-2.
BAUTE, P.B. (1980), Is the cure in the labelling?, 'Transactional Analysis Journal', vol.10, no.2, pp.118-20.
BERNE, E. (1961), 'Transactional Analysis in Psychotherapy', New York, Grove.
BERNE, E. (1966), 'Principles of Group Treatment', New York, Grove.
BERNE, E. (1967), 'Games People Play', London, Penguin.

BERNE, E. (1971), 'A Layman's Guide to Psychoanalysis', London, Penguin.

BERNE, E. (1972), 'What Do You Say After You Say Hello?', New York, Grove.

BERNE, E. (Steiner, C.M., ed.) (1976), 'Beyond Games and Scripts, a Selection of Major Writings', New York, Grove.

BIESTEK, F.P. (1961), 'The Casework Relationship', London, Unwin.

BOULTON, M. (1978), The Nurturing Parent and social issues, 'Transactional Analysis Journal', vol.8, no.2, pp.117-20.

BRANDON, D. (1976), 'Zen in the Art of Helping', London, Routledge & Kegan Paul.

BUTRYM, Z. (1976), 'The Nature of Social Work', London, Macmillan.

BYRON, A.J. (1976), Underworld Games, 'British Journal of Criminology', vol.16, no.3, pp.269-74.

CHARNY, I.W. (1974), The new psychotherapies and encounters of the seventies : progress or fads?, 'Humanist', vol.34, no.4, pp.34-9.

CLARE, A.W. with THOMPSON, S. (1981), 'Let's Talk About Me', London, BBC.

CLAYTON, S.H. and DUNBAR, R.L.M. (1977), Transactional analysis in an alcohol safety program, 'Social Work', May, pp.209-13.

CROSSMAN, P. (1963), Permission and protection, 'Transactional Analysis Bulletin', vol.5, no.19, pp.152-3.

DUSAY, J. (1977), 'Egograms', New York, Harper & Row.

ELIOT, T.S. (1936), 'Collected Poems', London, Faber & Faber.

ENGLISH, P. (1971 and 1972), Rackets and real feelings, 'Transactional Analysis Journal', vol.1, no.4 and vol.2, no.1, pp.225-30 and pp.23-5.

ERNST, F.H. (1971), The O K corral: the grid for get-on-with, 'Transactional Analysis Journal', vol.1, no.4, pp.33-42.

FALBERG, V. (1981), 'Attachment and Separation', London, British Agencies for Adoption and Fostering.

FALKOWSKI, D. et al. (1980), The assessment of ego states, 'British Journal of Psychiatry', vol.137, pp.572-3.

FORD, J. and HOLLICK, M. (1979), The singer or the song: an autobiographical account of a suicidal destructive person and her social worker, 'British Journal of Social Work', vol.9, no.4, pp.472-88.

FREED, A. (1971), 'Transactional Analysis for Kids', Sacramento, Jalmar.

FROMM, E. (1957), 'The Art of Loving', London, Unwin.

FROMM, E. (1978), 'To Have or To Be', London, Abacus.

FURLONG, F.W. (1977), The new psychotherapies: the courage to be, 'Canadian Psychiatric Association Journal', vol.22, pp.207-13.

GARBER, J. et al. (1976), A psycho-educational program for delinquent boys, 'Journal of Drug Addiction', vol.6, no.4, pp.331-41.

GELLERT, S.D. and WILSON, G. (1978), Family therapy, 'Transactional Analysis Journal', vol.8, no.1, pp.38-46.

GERE, F. (1975), Developing the O K miniscript, 'Transactional Analysis Journal', vol.5, no.3, pp.285-9.

GESSELL, A. et al. (1977), 'The Child from Five to Ten', New York, Harper & Row.

GILLESPIE, J.A. (1976), Feelings in the Adult ego state, 'Transactional Analysis Journal', vol.6, no.1, pp.69-72.

GOLDSTEIN, H. (1973), 'Social Work Practice - a Unitary Approach', Columbia, University of South Carolina.

GOULDING, R.L. (1974), Thinking and feeling in transactional analysis, 'Voices', vol.10, no.1, pp.11-13.

GOULDING, R.L. and GOULDING, M.M. (1976), Injunctions, decisions and redecisions, 'Transactional Analysis Journal', vol.6, no.1, pp.41-8.

HALE, B.J. et al. (1974), The use of transactional analysis and other tools in understanding drug activities, 'Journal of Drug Education', vol.4, no.2, pp.197-204.

HARRIS, T.A. (1973), 'I'm O K - You're O K', London, Pan.

HEYER, N.R. (1979), Development of a questionnaire to measure ego states, with some applications to social and comparative psychiatry, 'Transactional Analysis Journal', vol.9, no.1, pp.9-19.

HOLLOWAY, W.H. (1973), 'Clinical Transactional Analysis with Use of the Life Script Questionnaire', Aptos, CA, author.

JAMES, J. (1973), The game plan, 'Transactional Analysis Journal', vol.3, no.4, pp.14-17.

JAMES, M. (ed.) (1977), 'Techniques in Transactional Analysis', Reading, Mass., Addison-Wesley.

JAMES, M. and JONGEWARD, D. (1973a), 'Born to Win', Reading, Mass., Addison-Wesley.

JAMES, M. and JONGEWARD, D. (1973b), 'Winning with People', Reading, Mass., Addison-Wesley.

JAMES, M. and JONGEWARD, D. (1975), 'The People Book', Reading, Mass., Addison-Wesley.

JAMES, M. and SAVARY, L. (1977), 'A New Self', Reading, Mass., Addison-Wesley.

JESNESS, C.F. (1975), Comparative effectiveness of behaviour modification and transactional analysis, 'Journal of Consulting and Clinical Psychology', vol.43, no.6, pp.758-79.

JESNESS, C.F. et al. (1972), 'Youth Center Project', California Youth Authority.

JOINES, V.S. (1976), Differentiating structural and functional, 'Transactional Analysis Journal', vol.6, no.4, pp.377-9.

JORDAN, B. (1979), 'Helping in Social Work', London, Routledge & Kegan Paul.

JUSTICE, B. and JUSTICE, R. (1977), 'The Abusing Family', New York, Human Sciences.

JUSTICE, B. and JUSTICE, R. (1978), Evaluating outcome of group therapy for abusing parents, 'Corrective and Social Psychiatry and Journal of Behaviour Technology, Methods and Therapy', vol.24, no.1, pp.45-9.

KAHLER, T. (1975), Drivers, the key to the process of scripts, 'Transactional Analysis Journal', vol.5, no.3, pp.280-4.

KAHLER, T. and HEDGES, C. (1974), The miniscript, 'Transactional Analysis Journal', vol.4, no.1, pp.26-42.

KAPLAN, H. and SADCOCK, B.J, (1972), 'New Models for Group Therapy', New York, Dutton.

KARPMAN, S. (1968), Fairy tales and script drama analysis, 'Transactional Analysis Bulletin', vol.7, no.26, pp.39-43.

KARPMAN, S. (1971), Options, 'Transactional Analysis Journal', vol.1, no.1, pp.79-87.

KLEIN, M. (1980), 'Lives People Live', Chichester, Wiley.

KOVEL, J. (1978), 'A Complete Guide to Therapy', Harmondsworth, Pelican.

KRUMPER, M. (1977), Sub-dividing the Adult, 'Transactional Analysis Journal', vol.7, no.4, pp.298-9.

KUIJT, J. (1980), Differentiation of the Adult ego state, 'Transactional Analysis Journal', vol.10, no.3, pp.232-7.

LESTER, G.W. (1980), Transactional analysis marital therapy, 'Transactional Analysis Journal', vol.10, no.1, pp.33-6.

LEVIN, P. (1974), 'Becoming the Way We Are', Berkeley, California, author.

McCORMICK, P. (1971), 'Guide for the Use of a Life - Script Questionnaire in Transactional Analysis', San Francisco, International Transactional Analysis Association.

McDERMOTT, F.E. (ed.) (1975), 'Self-determination in Social Work', London, Routledge & Kegan Paul.

McKENNA, J. (1974), Stroking profile, 'Transactional Analysis Journal', vol.4, no.4, pp.20-4.

O'CONNOR, W. (1977), Some observations on the use of transactional analysis in marriage counselling, 'Journal of Marriage and Family Counselling', January, pp.27-34.

PINCUS, A. and MINAHAN, A. (1973), 'Social Work Practice: Model and Method', Illinois, Peacock.

PITMAN, E. (1981), Reparenting P_1 and P_2 aspects, 'Transactions', vol. Spring, pp.8-9.

PORTER, N. (1975), Functional analysis, 'Transactional Analysis Journal', vol.5, no.3, pp.272-3.

PROCTER, B. (1978), 'Counselling Shop', London, Deutsch.

RAGG, N.M. (1977), 'People Not Cases', London, Routledge & Kegan Paul.

REDDY, M. (1979), 'Handbook for Transactional Analysis Users', Woburn Sands, author.

REYNOLDS, D. (1979), T.A., What's your game?, 'Community Care', 12 July, pp.23-6.

ROBERTS, R.W. and NEE, R.H. (eds) (1970), 'Theories of Social Casework', Chicago, University of Chicago Press.

ROGERS, C.R. (1951), 'Client-Centred Therapy', London, Constable.

ROGERS, C.R. (1967), 'On Becoming a Person', London, Constable.

ROTH, R. (1977), Transactional Analysis in residential treatment of adolescents, 'Child Welfare', vol.LVI, no.1, pp.776-86.

SAGER, C.J. and KAPLAN, H.S. (1972), 'Progress in Group and Family Therapy', New York, Brunner/Mazel.

SCHIFF, J.L. (1969), Reparenting schizophrenics, 'Transactional Analysis Bulletin', vol.8, no.31, pp.47-63.

SCHIFF, J.L. (1975), 'Cathexis Reader', New York, Harper & Row.

SCHIFF, J.L. and DAY, B. (1970), 'All My Children', New York, Jove.

SPENCE, M.T. (1974), Group work with old people, 'Transactional Analysis Journal', vol.4, no.2, pp.35-7.

STEINER, C.M. (1971), 'Games Alcoholics Play', New York, Grove.

STEINER, C.M. (1974), 'Scripts People Live', New York, Grove.

SUTTON, C. (1979), 'Psychology for Social Workers and Counsellors, an Introduction', London, Routledge & Kegan Paul.

THOMSON, S.H. (1974), Insight for the sightless - a transactional analysis group for the blind, 'Transactional Analysis Journal', vol.4, no.1, pp.13-17.

THOMSON, S.H. and MOSHER, J.R. (1975), An eye to change: Transactional analysis in rehabilitation, 'New Outlook for the Blind', July, pp.64-72.

TOLSON, E.R. and REID, W.J. (eds) (1981), 'Models of Family Treatment', New York, University of Columbia Press.

TWEED, B. (1980), The use of transactional analysis with a psychotic client, 'Social Work Today', vol.11, no.24, pp.14-16.

WALROND-SKINNER, S. (ed.) (1979), 'Marital and Family Psychotherapy', London, Routledge & Kegan Paul.

WILSON, B.D. (1981), Doctoral dissertations on transactional analysis, 1963-1980, 'Transactional Analysis Journal', vol.11, no.3, pp.194-202.

WILSON, L. (1979), A case of T.A., 'Community Care', 12 July, pp.26-7.

WOLBERG, L.R. (ed.) (1967), 'The Techniques of Psychotherapy', New York, Grune and Stratton.

WOOLLAMS, S.J. et al. (1976), 'Transactional Analysis in
Brief', Ann Arbor, Huron Valley.
WOOLLAMS, S.J. and BROWN, M. (1979), 'Transactional
Analysis: the Total Handbook', New York, Prentice Hall.
WYCKHOFF, H. (ed.) (1979), 'Love, Therapy and Politics',
New York, Grove.

Index

Routledge Social Science Series

Routledge & Kegan Paul
London, Boston, Melbourne and Henley

39 Store Street, London WC1E 7DD
9 Park Street, Boston, Mass 02108
296 Beaconsfield Parade, Middle Park,
Melbourne, 3206 Australia
Broadway House, Newtown Road,
Henley-on-Thames, Oxon RG9 1EN

Contents

*Authors wishing to submit manuscripts for any series
in this catalogue should send them to the Social Science Editor,
Routledge & Kegan Paul plc, 39 Store Street,
London WC1E 7DD.*
● *Books so marked are available in paperback also.*
○ *Books so marked are available in paperback only.*
*All books are in metric Demy 8vo format (216 × 138mm approx.)
unless otherwise stated.*

2

International Library of Sociology
General Editor John Rex

GENERAL SOCIOLOGY

Alexander, J. Theoretical Logic in Sociology.
  Volume 1: Positivism, Presuppositions and Current Controversies. *234 pp.*
  Volume 2: The Antinomies of Classical Thought: *Marx and Durkheim.*
  Volume 3: The Classical Attempt at Theoretical Synthesis: *Max Weber.*
  Volume 4: The Modern Reconstruction of Classical Thought: *Talcott Parsons.*
Barnsley, J. H. The Social Reality of Ethics. *464 pp.*
Brown, Robert. Explanation in Social Science. *208 pp.*
● Rules and Laws in Sociology. *192 pp.*
Bruford, W. H. Chekhov and His Russia. *A Sociological Study. 244 pp.*
Burton, F. and **Carlen, P.** Official Discourse. *On Discourse Analysis, Government Publications, Ideology. 160 pp.*
Cain, Maureen E. Society and the Policeman's Role. *326 pp.*
● **Fletcher, Colin.** Beneath the Surface. *An Account of Three Styles of Sociological Research. 221 pp.*
Gibson, Quentin. The Logic of Social Enquiry. *240 pp.*
Glassner, B. Essential Interactionism. *208 pp.*
Glucksmann, M. Structuralist Analysis in Contemporary Social Thought. *212 pp.*
Gurvitch, Georges. Sociology of Law. *Foreword by Roscoe Pound. 264 pp.*
Hinkle, R. Founding Theory of American Sociology 1881–1913. *376 pp.*
Homans, George C. Sentiments and Activities. *336 pp.*
Johnson, Harry M. Sociology: *A Systematic Introduction. Foreword by Robert K. Merton. 710 pp.*
● **Keat, Russell** and **Urry, John.** Social Theory as Science. *Second Edition. 278 pp.*
Mannheim, Karl. Essays on Sociology and Social Psychology. *Edited by Paul Kecskemeti. With Editorial Note by Adolph Lowe. 344 pp.*
Martindale, Don. The Nature and Types of Sociological Theory. *292 pp.*
● **Maus, Heinz.** A Short History of Sociology. *234 pp.*
Merquior, J. G. Rousseau and Weber. *A Study in the Theory of Legitimacy. 240 pp.*
Myrdal, Gunnar. Value in Social Theory: *A Collection of Essays on Methodology. Edited by Paul Streeten. 332 pp.*
Ogburn, William F. and **Nimkoff, Meyer F.** A Handbook of Sociology. *Preface by Karl Mannheim. 656 pp. 46 figures. 35 tables.*
Parsons, Talcott and **Smelser, Neil J.** Economy and Society: *A Study in the Integration of Economic and Social Theory. 362 pp.*
Payne, G., Dingwall, R., Payne, J. and **Carter, M.** Sociology and Social Research. *336 pp.*
Podgórecki, A. Practical Social Sciences. *144 pp.*
Podgórecki, A. and **Łos, M.** Multidimensional Sociology. *268 pp.*
Raffel, S. Matters of Fact. *A Sociological Inquiry. 152 pp.*
● **Rex, John.** Key Problems of Sociological Theory. *220 pp.*
  Sociology and the Demystification of the Modern World. *282 pp.*
● **Rex, John.** (Ed.) Approaches to Sociology. *Contributions by Peter Abell, Frank Bechhofer, Basil Bernstein, Ronald Fletcher, David Frisby, Miriam Glucksmann, Peter Lassman, Herminio Martins, John Rex, Roland Robertson, John Westergaard and Jock Young. 302 pp.*
Rigby, A. Alternative Realities. *352 pp.*
Roche, M. Phenomenology, Language and the Social Sciences. *374 pp.*
Sahay, A. Sociological Analysis. *220 pp.*
Strasser, Hermann. The Normative Structure of Sociology. *Conservative and Emancipatory Themes in Social Thought. 286 pp.*

Strong, P. Ceremonial Order of the Clinic. *267 pp.*
Urry, J. Reference Groups and the Theory of Revolution. *244 pp.*
Weinberg, E. Development of Sociology in the Soviet Union. *173 pp.*

FOREIGN CLASSICS OF SOCIOLOGY

● **Gerth, H. H.** and **Mills, C. Wright.** From Max Weber: *Essays in Sociology.*
502 pp.
● **Tönnies, Ferdinand.** Community and Association (*Gemeinschaft und Gesell-schaft*). *Translated and Supplemented by Charles P. Loomis. Foreword by Pitirim A. Sorokin. 334 pp.*

SOCIAL STRUCTURE

Andreski, Stanislav. Military Organization and Society. *Foreword by Professor A. R. Radcliffe-Brown. 226 pp. 1 folder.*
Bozzoli, B. The Political Nature of a Ruling Class. *Capital and Ideology in South Africa 1890–1939. 396 pp.*
Bauman, Z. Memories of Class. *The Prehistory and After life of Class. 240 pp.*
Broom, L., Lancaster Jones, F., McDonnell, P. and **Williams, T.** The Inheritance of Inequality. *208 pp.*
Carlton, Eric. Ideology and Social Order. *Foreword by Professor Philip Abrahams. 326 pp.*
Clegg, S. and **Dunkerley, D.** Organization, Class and Control. *614 pp.*
Coontz, Sydney H. Population Theories and the Economic Interpretation. *202 pp.*
Coser, Lewis. The Functions of Social Conflict. *204 pp.*
Crook, I. and **D.** The First Years of the Yangyi Commune. *304 pp., illustrated.*
Dickie-Clark, H. F. Marginal Situation: *A Sociological Study of a Coloured Group. 240 pp. 11 tables.*
Fidler, J. The British Business Elite. *Its Attitudes to Class, Status and Power. 332 pp.*
Giner, S. and **Archer, M. S.** (Eds) Contemporary Europe: *Social Structures and Cultural Patterns. 336 pp.*
● **Glaser, Barney** and **Strauss, Anselm L.** Status Passage: *A Formal Theory. 212 pp.*
Glass, D. V. (Ed.) Social Mobility in Britain. *Contributions by J. Berent, T. Bottomore, R. C. Chambers, J. Floud, D. V. Glass, J. R. Hall, H. T. Himmelweit, R. K. Kelsall, F. M. Martin, C. A. Moser, R. Mukherjee and W. Ziegel. 420 pp.*
Kelsall, R. K. Higher Civil Servants in Britain: *From 1870 to the Present Day. 268 pp. 31 tables.*
● **Lawton, Denis.** Social Class, Language and Education. *192 pp.*
McLeish, John. The Theory of Social Change. *Four Views Considered. 128 pp.*
● **Marsh, David C.** The Changing Social Structure of England and Wales, 1871–1961. *Revised edition. 288 pp.*
Menzies, Ken. Talcott Parsons and the Social Image of Man. *206 pp.*
● **Mouzelis, Nicos.** Organization and Bureaucracy. *An Analysis of Modern Theories. 240 pp.*
● **Ossowski, Stanislav.** Class Structure in the Social Consciousness. *210 pp.*
● **Podgórecki, Adam.** Law and Society. *302 pp.*
Ratcliffe, P. Racism and Reaction. *A Profile of Handsworth. 388 pp.*
Renner, Karl. Institutions of Private Law and Their Social Functions. *Edited, with an Introduction and Notes, by O. Kahn-Freud. Translated by Agnes Schwarzschild. 316 pp.*
Rex, J. and **Tomlinson, S.** Colonial Immigrants in a British City. *A Class Analysis. 368 pp.*
Smooha, S. Israel. *Pluralism and Conflict. 472 pp.*
Strasser, H. and **Randall, S. C.** An Introduction to Theories of Social Change. *300 pp.*

Wesolowski, W. Class, Strata and Power. *Trans. and with Introduction by G. Kolankiewicz. 160 pp.*

Zureik, E. Palestinians in Israel. *A Study in Internal Colonialism. 264 pp.*

SOCIOLOGY AND POLITICS

Acton, T. A. Gypsy Politics and Social Change. *316 pp.*

Burton, F. Politics of Legitimacy. *Struggles in a Belfast Community. 250 pp.*

Crook, I. and D. Revolution in a Chinese Village. *Ten Mile Inn. 216 pp., illustrated.*

de Silva, S. B. D. The Political Economy of Underdevelopment. *640 pp.*

Etzioni-Halevy, E. Political Manipulation and Administrative Power. *A Comparative Study. 228 pp.*

Fielding, N. The National Front. *260 pp.*

● Hechter, Michael. Internal Colonialism. *The Celtic Fringe in British National Development, 1536–1966. 380 pp.*

Levy, N. The Foundations of the South African Cheap Labour System. *367 pp.*

Kornhauser, William. The Politics of Mass Society. *272 pp. 20 tables.*

● Korpi, W. The Working Class in Welfare Capitalism. *Work, Unions and Politics in Sweden. 472 pp.*

Kroes, R. Soldiers and Students. *A Study of Right- and Left-wing Students. 174 pp.*

Martin, Roderick. Sociology of Power. *214 pp.*

Merquior, J. G. Rousseau and Weber. *A Study in the Theory of Legitimacy. 286 pp.*

Myrdal, Gunnar. The Political Element in the Development of Economic Theory. *Translated from the German by Paul Streeten. 282 pp.*

Preston, P. W. Theories of Development. *296 pp.*

Varma, B. N. The Sociology and Politics of Development. *A Theoretical Study. 236 pp.*

Wong, S.-L. Sociology and Socialism in Contemporary China. *160 pp.*

Wootton, Graham. Workers, Unions and the State. *188 pp.*

CRIMINOLOGY

Ancel, Marc. Social Defence: *A Modern Approach to Criminal Problems. Foreword by Leon Radzinowicz. 240 pp.*

Athens, L. Violent Criminal Acts and Actors. *104 pp.*

Cain, Maureen E. Society and the Policeman's Role. *326 pp.*

Cloward, Richard A. and Ohlin, Lloyd E. Delinquency and Opportunity: *A Theory of Delinquent Gangs. 248 pp.*

Downes, David M. The Delinquent Solution. *A Study in Subcultural Theory. 296 pp.*

Friedlander, Kate. The Psycho-Analytical Approach to Juvenile Delinquency: *Theory, Case Studies, Treatment. 320 pp.*

Gleuck, Sheldon and Eleanor. Family Environment and Delinquency. *With the statistical assistance of Rose W. Kneznek. 340 pp.*

Lopez-Rey, Manuel. Crime. *An Analytical Appraisal. 288 pp.*

Mannheim, Hermann. Comparative Criminology: *A Text Book. Two volumes. 442 pp. and 380 pp.*

Morris, Terence. The Criminal Area: *A Study in Social Ecology. Foreword by Hermann Mannheim. 232 pp. 25 tables. 4 maps.*

Rock, Paul. Making People Pay. *338 pp.*

● Taylor, Ian, Walton, Paul and Young, Jock. The New Criminology. *For a Social Theory of Deviance. 325 pp.*

● Taylor, Ian, Walton, Paul and Young, Jock. (Eds) Critical Criminology. *268 pp.*

SOCIAL PSYCHOLOGY

Bagley, Christopher. The Social Psychology of the Epileptic Child. *320 pp.*
Brittan, Arthur. Meanings and Situations. *224 pp.*
Carroll, J. Break-Out from the Crystal Palace. *200 pp.*
● **Fleming, C. M.** Adolescence: Its Social Psychology. *With an Introduction to recent findings from the fields of Anthropology, Physiology, Medicine, Psychometrics and Sociometry. 288 pp.*
● The Social Psychology of Education: *An Introduction and Guide to Its Study. 136 pp.*
Linton, Ralph. The Cultural Background of Personality. *132 pp.*
● **Mayo, Elton.** The Social Problems of an Industrial Civilization. *With an Appendix on the Political Problem. 180 pp.*
Ottaway, A. K. C. Learning Through Group Experience. *176 pp.*
Plummer, Ken. Sexual Stigma. *An Interactionist Account. 254 pp.*
● **Rose, Arnold M.** (Ed.) Human Behaviour and Social Processes: *an Interactionist Approach. Contributions by Arnold M. Rose, Ralph H. Turner, Anselm Strauss, Everett C. Hughes, E. Franklin Frazier, Howard S. Becker et al. 696 pp.*
Smelser, Neil J. Theory of Collective Behaviour. *448 pp.*
Stephenson, Geoffrey M. The Development of Conscience. *128 pp.*
Young, Kimball. Handbook of Social Psychology. *658 pp. 16 figures. 10 tables.*

SOCIOLOGY OF THE FAMILY

Bell, Colin R. Middle Class Families: *Social and Geographical Mobility. 224 pp.*
Burton, Lindy. Vulnerable Children. *272 pp.*
Gavron, Hannah. The Captive Wife: *Conflicts of Household Mothers. 190 pp.*
George, Victor and **Wilding, Paul.** Motherless Families. *248 pp.*
Klein, Josephine. Samples from English Cultures.
    1. Three Preliminary Studies and Aspects of Adult Life in England. *447 pp.*
    2. Child-Rearing Practices and Index. *247 pp.*
Klein, Viola. The Feminine Character. *History of an Ideology. 244 pp.*
McWhinnie, Alexina M. Adopted Children. *How They Grow Up. 304 pp.*
● **Morgan, D. H. J.** Social Theory and the Family. *188 pp.*
● **Myrdal, Alva** and **Klein, Viola.** Women's Two Roles: *Home and Work. 238 pp. 27 tables.*
Parsons, Talcott and **Bales, Robert F.** Family: Socialization and Interaction Process. *In collaboration with James Olds, Morris Zelditch and Philip E. Slater. 456 pp. 50 figures and tables.*

SOCIAL SERVICES

Bastide, Roger. The Sociology of Mental Disorder. *Translated from the French by Jean McNeil. 260 pp.*
Carlebach, Julius. Caring for Children in Trouble. *266 pp.*
George, Victor. Foster Care. *Theory and Practice. 234 pp.*
    Social Security: *Beveridge and After. 258 pp.*
George, V. and **Wilding, P.** Motherless Families. *248 pp.*
● **Goetschius, George W.** Working with Community Groups. *256 pp.*
Goetschius, George W. and **Tash, Joan.** Working with Unattached Youth. *416 pp.*
Heywood, Jean S. Children in Care. *The Development of the Service for the Deprived Child. Third revised edition. 284 pp.*
King, Roy D., Ranes, Norma V. and **Tizard, Jack.** Patterns of Residential Care. *356 pp.*
Leigh, John. Young People and Leisure. *256 pp.*
● **Mays, John.** (Ed.) Penelope Hall's Social Services of England and Wales. *368 pp.*

Morris Mary. Voluntary Work and the Welfare State. *300 pp.*
Nokes. P. L. The Professional Task in Welfare Practice. *152 pp.*
Timms, Noel. Psychiatric Social Work in Great Britain (1939–1962). *280 pp.*
● Social Casework: *Principles and Practice. 256 pp.*

SOCIOLOGY OF EDUCATION

Banks, Olive. Parity and Prestige in English Secondary Education: a Study in
    Educational Sociology. *272 pp.*
● Blyth, W. A. L. English Primary Education. *A Sociological Description.*
    2. Background. *168 pp.*
Collier, K. G. The Social Purposes of Education: *Personal and Social Values in
    Education. 268 pp.*
Evans, K. M. Sociometry and Education. *158 pp.*
● Ford, Julienne. Social Class and the Comprehensive School. *192 pp.*
Foster, P. J. Education and Social Change in Ghana. *336 pp. 3 maps.*
Fraser, W. R. Education and Society in Modern France. *150 pp.*
Grace, Gerald R. Role Conflict and the Teacher. *150 pp.*
Hans, Nicholas. New Trends in Education in the Eighteenth Century. *278 pp.*
    19 tables.
●   Comparative Education: *A Study of Educational Factors and Traditions. 360 pp.*
● Hargreaves, David. Interpersonal Relations and Education. *432 pp.*
●   Social Relations in a Secondary School. *240 pp.*
    School Organization and Pupil Involvement. *A Study of Secondary Schools.*
● Mannheim, Karl and Stewart, W. A. C. An Introduction to the Sociology of
    Education. *206 pp.*
● Musgrove, F. Youth and the Social Order. *176 pp.*
● Ottaway, A. K. C. Education and Society: An Introduction to the Sociology of
    Education. *With an Introduction by W. O. Lester Smith. 212 pp.*
Peers, Robert. Adult Education: *A Comparative Study. Revised edition. 398 pp.*
Stratta, Erica. The Education of Borstal Boys. *A Study of their Educational
    Experiences prior to, and during, Borstal Training. 256 pp.*
● Taylor, P. H., Reid, W. A. and Holley, B. J. The English Sixth Form. *A Case
    Study in Curriculum Research. 198 pp.*

SOCIOLOGY OF CULTURE

● Eppel, E. M. and M. Adolescents and Morality: *A Study of some Moral Values
    and Dilemmas of Working Adolescents in the Context of a changing Climate
    of Opinion. Foreword by W. J. H. Sprott. 268 pp. 39 tables.*
● Fromm, Erich. The Fear of Freedom. *286 pp.*
●   The Sane Society. *400 pp.*
Johnson, L. The Cultural Critics. *From Matthew Arnold to Raymond Williams.*
    233 pp.
Mannheim, Karl. Essays on the Sociology of Culture. *Edited by Ernst
    Mannheim in co-operation with Paul Kecskemeti. Editorial Note by Adolph
    Lowe. 280 pp.*
    Structures of Thinking. *Edited by David Kettler, Volker Meja and Nico Stehr.*
    304 pp.
Merquior, J. G. The Veil and the Mask. *Essays on Culture and Ideology.
    Foreword by Ernest Gellner. 140 pp.*
Zijderfeld, A. C. On Clichés. *The Supersedure of Meaning by Function in
    Modernity. 150 pp.*
    Reality in a Looking Glass. *Rationality through an Analysis of Traditional
    Folly. 208 pp.*

SOCIOLOGY OF RELIGION

Argyle, Michael and **Beit-Hallahmi, Benjamin.** The Social Psychology of Religion. *256 pp.*

Glasner, Peter E. The Sociology of Secularisation. *A Critique of a Concept. 146 pp.*

Hall, J. R. The Ways Out. *Utopian Communal Groups in an Age of Babylon. 280 pp.*

Ranson, S., Hinings, B. and **Bryman, A.** Clergy, Ministers and Priests. *216 pp.*

Stark, Werner. The Sociology of Religion. *A Study of Christendom.*
Volume II. *Sectarian Religion. 368 pp.*
Volume III. *The Universal Church. 464 pp.*
Volume IV. *Types of Religious Man. 352 pp.*
Volume V. *Types of Religious Culture. 464 pp.*

Turner, B. S. Weber and Islam. *216 pp.*

Watt, W. Montgomery. Islam and the Integration of Society. 230 pp.

Pomian-Srzednicki, M. Religious Change in Contemporary Poland. *Sociology and Secularization. 280 pp.*

SOCIOLOGY OF ART AND LITERATURE

Jarvie, Ian C. Towards a Sociology of the Cinema. *A Comparative Essay on the Structure and Functioning of a Major Entertainment Industry. 405 pp.*

Rust, Frances S. Dance in Society. *An Analysis of the Relationships between the Social Dance and Society in England from the Middle Ages to the Present Day. 256 pp. 8 pp. of plates.*

Schücking, L. L. The Sociology of Literary Taste. *112 pp.*

Wolff, Janet. Hermeneutic Philosophy and the Sociology of Art. *150 pp.*

SOCIOLOGY OF KNOWLEDGE

Diesing, P. Patterns of Discovery in the Social Sciences. *262 pp.*

● **Douglas, J. D.** (Ed.) Understanding Everyday Life. *270 pp.*

● **Hamilton, P.** Knowledge and Social Structure. *174 pp.*

Jarvie, I. C. Concepts and Society. *232 pp.*

Mannheim, Karl. Essays on the Sociology of Knowledge. *Edited by Paul Kecskemeti. Editorial Note by Adolph Lowe. 353 pp.*

Remmling, Gunter W. The Sociology of Karl Mannheim. *With a Bibliographical Guide to the Sociology of Knowledge, Ideological Analysis, and Social Planning. 255 pp.*

Remmling, Gunter W. (Ed.) Towards the Sociology of Knowledge. *Origin and Development of a Sociological Thought Style. 463 pp.*

Scheler, M. Problems of a Sociology of Knowledge. *Trans. by M. S. Frings. Edited and with an Introduction by K. Stikkers. 232 pp.*

URBAN SOCIOLOGY

Aldridge, M. The British New Towns. *A Programme Without a Policy. 232 pp.*

Ashworth, William. The Genesis of Modern British Town Planning: *A Study in Economic and Social History of the Nineteenth and Twentieth Centuries. 288 pp.*

Brittan, A. The Privatised World. *196 pp.*

Cullingworth, J. B. Housing Needs and Planning Policy: *a Restatement of the Problems of Housing Need and 'Overspill' in England and Wales. 232 pp. 44 tables. 8 maps.*

Dickinson, Robert E. City and Region: *A Geographical Interpretation. 608 pp. 125 figures.*

The West European City: *A Geographical Interpretation. 600 pp. 129 maps. 29 plates.*

Humphreys, Alexander J. New Dubliners: *Urbanization and the Irish Family.* *Foreword by George C. Homans. 304 pp.*

Jackson, Brian. Working Class Community: *Some General Notions raised by a Series of Studies in Northern England. 192 pp.*

● **Mann, P. H.** An Approach to Urban Sociology. *240 pp.*

Mellor, J. R. Urban Sociology in an Urbanized Society. *326 pp.*

Morris, R. N. and **Mogey, J.** The Sociology of Housing. *Studies at Berinsfield. 232 pp. 4 pp. plates.*

Mullan, R. Stevenage Ltd. *438 pp.*

Rex, J. and **Tomlinson, S.** Colonial Immigrants in a British City. *A Class Analysis. 368 pp.*

Rosser, C. and **Harris, C.** The Family and Social Change. *A Study of Family and Kinship in a South Wales Town. 352 pp. 8 maps.*

● **Stacey, Margaret, Batsone, Eric, Bell, Colin** and **Thurcott, Anne.** Power, Persistence and Change. *A Second Study of Banbury. 196 pp.*

RURAL SOCIOLOGY

● **Mayer, Adrian C.** Peasants in the Pacific. *A Study of Fiji Indian Rural Society. 248 pp. 20 plates.*

Williams, W. M. The Sociology of an English Village: *Gosforth. 272 pp. 12 figures. 13 tables.*

SOCIOLOGY OF INDUSTRY AND DISTRIBUTION

Dunkerley, David. The Foreman. *Aspects of Task and Structure. 192 pp.*

Eldridge, J. E. T. *Industrial Disputes. Essays in the Sociology of Industrial Relations. 288 pp.*

Hollowell, Peter G. The Lorry Driver. *272 pp.*

● **Oxaal, I., Barnett, T.** and **Booth, D.** (Eds) Beyond the Sociology of Development. *Economy and Society in Latin America and Africa. 295 pp.*

Smelser, Neil J. Social Change in the Industrial Revolution: *An Application of Theory to the Lancashire Cotton Industry, 1770–1840. 468 pp. 12 figures. 14 tables.*

Watson, T. J. The Personnel Managers. *A Study in the Sociology of Work and Employment, 262 pp.*

ANTHROPOLOGY

Brandel-Syrier, Mia. Reeftown Elite. *A Study of Social Mobility in a Modern African Community on the Reef. 376 pp.*

Dickie-Clark, H. F. The Marginal Situation. *A Sociological Study of a Coloured Group. 236 pp.*

Dube, S. C. Indian Village. *Foreword by Morris Edward Opler. 276 pp. 4 plates.*

India's Changing Villages: *Human Factors in Community Development. 260 pp. 8 plates. 1 map.*

Fei, H.-T. Peasant Life in China. *A Field Study of Country Life in the Yangtze Valley. With a foreword by Bronislaw Malinowski. 328 pp. 16 pp. plates.*

Firth, Raymond. Malay Fishermen. *Their Peasant Economy. 420 pp. 17 pp. plates.*

Gulliver, P. H. Social Control in an African Society: a Study of the Arusha, Agricultural Masai of Northern Tanganykia. *320 pp. 8 plates. 10 figures.*

Family Herds. *288 pp.*

Jarvie, Ian C. The Revolution in Anthropology. *268 pp.*

Little, Kenneth L. Mende of Sierra Leone. *308 pp. and folder.*

Negroes in Britain. *With a New Introduction and Contemporary Study by Leonard Bloom. 320 pp.*

Tambs-Lyche, H. London Patidars. *168 pp.*
Madan, G. R. Western Sociologists on Indian Society. *Marx, Spencer, Weber, Durkheim, Pareto. 384 pp.*
Mayer, A. C. Peasants in the Pacific. *A Study of Fiji Indian Rural Society. 248 pp.*
Meer, Fatima. Race and Suicide in South Africa. *325 pp.*
Smith, Raymond T. The Negro Family in British Guiana: *Family Structure and Social Status in the Villages. With a Foreword by Meyer Fortes. 314 pp. 8 plates. 1 figure. 4 maps.*

SOCIOLOGY AND PHILOSOPHY

● **Adriaansens, H.** Talcott Parsons and the Conceptual Dilemma. *200 pp.*
Barnsley, John H. The Social Reality of Ethics. *A Comparative Analysis of Moral Codes. 448 pp.*
Diesing, Paul. Patterns of Discovery in the Social Sciences. *362 pp.*
● **Douglas, Jack D.** (Ed.) Understanding Everyday Life. *Toward the Reconstruction of Sociological Knowledge. Contributions by Alan F. Blum, Aaron W. Cicourel, Norman K. Denzin, Jack D. Douglas, John Heeren, Peter McHugh, Peter K. Manning, Melvin Power, Matthew Speier, Roy Turner, D. Lawrence Wieder, Thomas P. Wilson and Don H. Zimmerman. 370 pp.*
Gorman, Robert A. The Dual Vision. *Alfred Schutz and the Myth of Phenomenological Social Science. 240 pp.*
Jarvie, Ian C. Concepts and Society. *216 pp.*
Kilminster, R. Praxis and Method. *A Sociological Dialogue with Lukács, Gramsci and the Early Frankfurt School. 334 pp.*
Outhwaite, W. Concept Formation in Social Science. *255 pp.*
● **Pelz, Werner.** The Scope of Understanding in Sociology. *Towards a More Radical Reorientation in the Social Humanistic Sciences. 283 pp.*
Roche, Maurice, Phenomenology, Language and the Social Sciences. *371 pp.*
Sahay, Arun. Sociological Analysis. *212 pp.*
● **Slater, P.** Origin and Significance of the Frankfurt School. *A Marxist Perspective. 185 pp.*
Spurling, L. Phenomenology and the Social World. *The Philosophy of Merleau-Ponty and its Relation to the Social Sciences. 222 pp.*
Wilson, H. T. The American Ideology. *Science, Technology and Organization as Modes of Rationality. 368 pp.*

International Library of Anthropology
General Editor Adam Kuper

● **Ahmed, A. S.** Millennium and Charisma Among Pathans. *A Critical Essay in Social Anthropology. 192 pp.*
Pukhtun Economy and Society. *Traditional Structure and Economic Development. 422 pp.*
Barth, F. Selected Essays. *Volume 1. 256 pp.* Selected Essays. *Volume II. 200 pp.*
Brown, Paula. The Chimbu. *A Study of Change in the New Guinea Highlands. 151 pp.*
Duller, H. J. Development Technology. *192 pp.*
Foner, N. Jamaica Farewell. *200 pp.*
Gudeman, Stephen. Relationships, Residence and the Individual. *A Rural Panamanian Community. 288 pp. 11 plates, 5 figures, 2 maps, 10 tables.*
The Demise of a Rural Economy. *From Subsistence to Capitalism in a Latin American Village. 160 pp.*

Hamnett, Ian. Chieftainship and Legitimacy. *An Anthropological Study of Executive Law in Lesotho. 163 pp.*
Hanson, F. Allan. Meaning in Culture. *127 pp.*
Hazan, H. The Limbo People. *A Study of the Constitution of the Time Universe Among the Aged. 208 pp.*
Humphreys, S. C. Anthropology and the Greeks. *288 pp.*
Karp, I. Fields of Change Among the Iteso of Kenya. *140 pp.*
Kuper, A. Wives for Cattle. *Bridewealth in Southern Africa. 224 pp.*
Lloyd, P. C. Power and Independence. *Urban Africans' Perception of Social Inequality. 264 pp.*
Malinowski, B. and **de la Fuente, J.** Malinowski in Mexico. *The Economics of a Mexican Market System. Edited and Introduced by Susan Drucker-Brown. About 240 pp.*
Parry, J. P. Caste and Kinship in Kangra. *352 pp. Illustrated.*
Pettigrew, Joyce. Robber Noblemen. *A Study of the Political System of the Sikh Jats. 284 pp.*
Street, Brian V. The Savage in Literature. *Representations of 'Primitive' Society in English Fiction, 1858–1920. 207 pp.*
Van Den Berghe, Pierre L. Power and Privilege at an African University. *278 pp.*

International Library of Phenomenology and Moral Sciences
General Editor John O'Neill

Adorno, T. W. Aesthetic Theory. Translated by C. Lenhardt.
Apel, K.-O. Towards a Transformation of Philosophy. *308 pp.*
Bologh, R. W. Dialectical Phenomenology. *Marx's Method. 287 pp.*
Fekete, J. The Critical Twilight. *Explorations in the Ideology of Anglo-American Literary Theory from Eliot to McLuhan. 300 pp.*
Green, B. S. Knowing the Poor. *A Case Study in Textual Reality Construction. 200 pp.*
McHoul, A. W. How Texts Talk. *Essays on Reading and Ethnomethodology. 163 pp.*
Medina, A. Reflection, Time and the Novel. *Towards a Communicative Theory of Literature. 143 pp.*
O'Neill, J. Essaying Montaigne. *A Study of the Renaissance Institution of Writing and Reading. 244 pp.*
Schutz. A. Life Forms and Meaning Structure. *Translated, Introduced and Annotated by Helmut Wagner. 207 pp.*

International Library of Social Policy
General Editor Kathleen Jones

Bayley, M. Mental Handicap and Community Care. *426 pp.*
Bottoms, A. E. and **McClean, J. D.** Defendants in the Criminal Process. *284 pp.*
Bradshaw, J. The Family Fund. *An Initiative in Social Policy. 248 pp.*
Butler, J. R. Family Doctors and Public Policy. *208 pp.*
Davies, Martin. Prisoners of Society. *Attitudes and Aftercare. 204 pp.*
Gittus, Elizabeth. Flats, Families and the Under-Fives. *285 pp.*
Holman, Robert. Trading in Children. *A Study of Private Fostering. 355 pp.*
Jeffs, A. Young People and the Youth Service. *160 pp.*
Jones, Howard and **Cornes, Paul.** Open Prisons. *288 pp.*
Jones, Kathleen. History of the Mental Health Service. *428 pp.*

Jones, Kathleen with Brown, John, Cunningham, W. J., Roberts, Julian and
Williams, Peter. Opening the Door. *A Study of New Policies for the
Mentally Handicapped. 278 pp.*

Karn, Valerie. Retiring to the Seaside. *400 pp. 2 maps. Numerous tables.*

King, R. D. and Elliot, K. W. Albany: Birth of a Prison—End of an Era.
294 pp.

Thomas, J. E. The English Prison Officer since 1850. *258 pp.*

Walton, R. G. Women in Social Work. *303 pp.*

● Woodward, J. To Do the Sick No Harm. *A Study of the British Voluntary
Hospital System to 1875. 234 pp.*

International Library of Welfare and Philosophy
General Editors Noel Timms and David Watson

○ Campbell, J. The Left and Rights. *A Conceptual Analysis of the Idea of
Socialist Rights. About 296 pp.*

● McDermott, F. E. (Ed.) Self-Determination in Social Work. *A Collection of
Essays on Self-determination and Related Concepts by Philosophers and
Social Work Theorists. Contributors: F. P. Biestek, S. Bernstein, A. Keith-
Lucas, D. Sayer, H. H. Perelman, C. Whittington, R. F. Stalley, F. E.
McDermott, I. Berlin, H. J. McCloskey, H. L. A. Hart, J. Wilson, A. I.
Melden, S. I. Benn. 254 pp.*

● Plant, Raymond. Community and Ideology. *104 pp.*

● Plant, Raymond, Lesser, Harry and Taylor-Gooby, Peter. Political Philosophy
and Social Welfare. *Essays on the Normative Basis of Welfare Provision.
276 pp.*

Ragg, N. M. People Not Cases. *A Philosophical Approach to Social Work.
168 pp.*

Timms, Noel (Ed.) Social Welfare. *Why and How? 316 pp. 7 figures.*

● Timms, Noel and Watson, David (Eds) Talking About Welfare. *Readings in
Philosophy and Social Policy. Contributors: T. H. Marshall, R. B. Brandt,
G. H. von Wright, K. Nielsen, M. Cranston, R. M. Titmuss, R. S. Downie,
E. Telfer, D. Donnison, J. Benson, P. Leonard. A. Keith-Lucas, D. Walsh,
I. T. Ramsey. 230 pp.*

● Philosophy in Social Work. *250 pp.*

● Weale, A. Equality and Social Policy. *164 pp.*

Library of Social Work
General Editor Noel Timms

● Baldock, Peter. Community Work and Social Work. *140 pp.*

○ Beedell, Christopher. Residential Life with Children. *210 pp. Crown 8vo.*

● Berry, Juliet. Daily Experience in Residential Life. *A Study of Children and
their Care-givers. 202 pp.*

○ Social Work with Children. *190 pp. Crown 8vo.*

● Brearley, C. Paul. Residential Work with the Elderly. *116 pp.*

● Social Work, Ageing and Society. *126 pp.*

● Cheetham, Juliet. Social Work with Immigrants. *240 pp. Crown 8vo.*

● Cross, Crispin P. (Ed.) Interviewing and Communication in Social Work.
*Contributions by C. P. Cross, D. Laurenson, B. Strutt, S. Raven. 192 pp.
Crown 8vo.*

● Curnock, Kathleen and Hardiker, Pauline. Towards Practice Theory. *Skills and
Methods in Social Assessments. 208 pp.*

● Davies, Bernard. The Use of Groups in Social Work Practice. *158 pp.*

Davies, Bleddyn and Knapp, M. Old People's Homes and the Production of
Welfare. *264 pp.*

● **Davies, Martin.** Support Systems in Social Work. *144 pp.*
Ellis, June. (Ed.) West African Families in Britain. *A Meeting of Two Cultures. Contributions by Pat Stapleton, Vivien Biggs. 150 pp. 1 map.*
○ **Ford, J.** Human Behaviour. *Towards a Practical Understanding. About 160 pp.*
● **Hart, John.** Social Work and Sexual Conduct. *230 pp.*
Heraud, Brian. Training for Uncertainty. *A Sociological Approach to Social Work Education. 138 pp.*
Holder, D. and **Wardle, M.** Teamwork and the Development of a Unitary Approach. *212 pp.*
● **Hutten, Joan M.** Short-Term Contracts in Social Work. *Contributions by Stella M. Hall, Elsie Osborne, Mannie Sher, Eva Sternberg, Elizabeth Tuters. 134 pp.*
Jackson, Michael P. and **Valencia, B. Michael.** Financial Aid Through Social Work. *140 pp.*
◐ **Jones, Howard.** The Residential Community. *A Setting for Social Work. 150 pp.*
● (Ed.) Towards a New Social Work. *Contributions by Howard Jones, D. A. Fowler, J. R. Cypher, R. G. Walton, Geoffrey Mungham, Philip Priestley, Ian Shaw, M. Bartley, R. Deacon, Irwin Epstein, Geoffrey Pearson. 184 pp.*
Jones, Ray and **Pritchard, Colin.** (Eds) Social Work With Adolescents. *Contributions by Ray Jones, Colin Pritchard, Jack Dunham, Florence Rossetti, Andrew Kerslake, John Burns, William Gregory, Graham Templeman, Kenneth E. Reid, Audrey Taylor.*
○ **Jordon, William.** The Social Worker in Family Situations. *160 pp. Crown 8vo.*
◐ **Laycock, A. L.** Adolescents and Social Work. *128 pp. Crown 8vo.*
◐ **Lees, Ray.** Politics and Social Work. *128 pp. Crown 8vo.*
◐ Research Strategies for Social Welfare. *112 pp. Tables.*
○ **McCullough, M. K.** and **Ely, Peter J.** Social Work with Groups. *127 pp. Crown 8vo.*
● **Moffett, Jonathan.** Concepts in Casework Treatment. *128 pp. Crown 8vo.*
Parsloe, Phyllida. Juvenile Justice in Britain and the United States. *The Balance of Needs and Rights. 336 pp.*
◐ **Plant, Raymond.** Social and Moral Theory in Casework. *112 pp. Crown 8vo.*
Priestley, Philip, Fears, Denise and **Fuller, Roger.** Justice for Juveniles. *The 1969 Children and Young Persons Act: A Case for Reform? 128 pp.*
● **Pritchard, Colin** and **Taylor, Richard.** Social Work: Reform or Revolution? *170 pp.*
○ **Pugh, Elisabeth.** Social Work in Child Care. *128 pp. Crown 8vo.*
● **Robinson, Margaret.** Schools and Social Work. *282 pp.*
○ **Ruddock, Ralph.** Roles and Relationships. *128 pp. Crown 8vo.*
● **Sainsbury, Eric.** Social Diagnosis in Casework. *118 pp. Crown 8vo.*
● **Sainsbury, Eric, Phillips, David** and **Nixon, Stephen.** Social Work in Focus. *Clients' and Social Workers' Perceptions in Long-Term Social Work. 220 pp.*
● Social Work with Families. *Perceptions of Social Casework among Clients of a Family Service. 188pp.*
Seed, Philip. The Expansion of Social Work in Britain. *128 pp. Crown 8vo.*
◐ **Shaw, John.** The Self in Social Work. *124 pp.*
Smale, Gerald G. Prophecy, Behaviour and Change. *An Examination of Self-fulfilling Prophecies in Helping Relationships. 116 pp. Crown 8vo.*
Smith, Gilbert. Social Need. *Policy, Practice and Research. 155 pp.*
● Social Work and the Sociology of Organisations. *124 pp. Revised edition.*
● **Sutton, Carole.** Psychology for Social Workers and Counsellors. *An Introduction. 248 pp.*
◐ **Timms, Noel.** Language of Social Casework. *122 pp. Crown 8vo.*

● Recording in Social Work. *124 pp. Crown 8vo.*
● **Todd, F. Joan.** Social Work with the Mentally Subnormal. *96 pp. Crown 8vo.*
⊕ **Walrond-Skinner, Sue.** Family Therapy. *The Treatment of Natural Systems. 172 pp.*
● **Warham, Joyce.** An Introduction to Administration for Social Workers. *Revised edition. 112 pp.*
● An Open Case. *The Organisational Context of Social Work. 172 pp.*
○ **Wittenberg, Isca Salzberger.** Psycho-Analytic Insight and Relationships. *A Kleinian Approach. 196 pp. Crown 8vo.*

Primary Socialization, Language and Education
General Editor Basil Bernstein

Adlam, Diana S., *with the assistance of Geoffrey Turner and Lesley Lineker.* Code in Context. *272 pp.*
Bernstein, Basil. Class, Codes and Control. *3 volumes.*
●   1. *Theoretical Studies Towards a Sociology of Language. 254 pp.*
    2. *Applied Studies Towards a Sociology of Language. 377 pp.*
●   3. *Towards a Theory of Educational Transmission. 167 pp.*
Brandis, Walter and **Henderson, Dorothy.** Social Class, Language and Communication. *288 pp.*
Cook-Gumperz, Jenny. Social Control and Socialization. *A Study of Class Differences in the Language of Maternal Control. 290 pp.*
● **Gahagan, D. M.** and **G. A.** Talk Reform. *Exploration in Language for Infant School Children. 160 pp.*
Hawkins, P. R. Social Class, the Nominal Group and Verbal Strategies. *About 220 pp.*
Robinson, W. P. and **Rakstraw, Susan D. A.** A Question of Answers. *2 volumes. 192 pp. and 180 pp.*
Turner, Geoffrey J. and **Mohan, Bernard A.** A Linguistic Description and Computer Programme for Children's Speech. *208 pp.*

Reports of the Institute of Community Studies

Baker, J. The Neighbourhood Advice Centre. *A Community Project in Camden. 320 pp.*
● **Cartwright, Ann.** Patients and their Doctors. *A Study of General Practice. 304 pp.*
Dench, Geoff. Maltese in London. *A Case-study in the Erosion of Ethnic Consciousness. 302 pp.*
Jackson, Brian and **Marsden, Dennis.** Education and the Working Class: *Some General Themes Raised by a Study of 88 Working-class Children in a Northern Industrial City. 268 pp. 2 folders.*
Madge, C. and **Willmott, P.** Inner City Poverty in Paris and London. *144 pp.*
Marris, Peter. The Experience of Higher Education. *232 pp. 27 tables.*
● Loss and Change. *192 pp.*
Marris, Peter and **Rein, Martin.** Dilemmas of Social Reform. *Poverty and Community Action in the United States. 256 pp.*
Marris, Peter and **Somerset, Anthony.** African Businessmen. *A Study of Entrepreneurship and Development in Kenya. 256 pp.*
Mills, Richard. Young Outsiders: *a Study in Alternative Communities. 216 pp.*
Runciman, W. G. Relative Deprivation and Social Justice. *A Study of Attitudes to Social Inequality in Twentieth-Century England. 352 pp.*

Willmott, Peter. Adolescent Boys in East London. *230 pp.*
Willmott, Peter and **Young, Michael.** Family and Class in a London Suburb. *202 pp. 47 tables.*
Young, Michael and **McGeeney, Patrick.** Learning Begins at Home. *A Study of a Junior School and its Parents. 128 pp.*
Young, Michael and **Willmott, Peter.** Family and Kinship in East London. *Foreword by Richard M. Titmuss. 252 pp. 39 tables.*
The Symmetrical Family. *410 pp.*

Reports of the Institute for Social Studies in Medical Care

Cartwright, Ann, Hockey, Lisbeth and **Anderson, John J.** Life Before Death. *310 pp.*
Dunnell, Karen and **Cartwright, Ann.** Medicine Takers, Prescribers and Hoarders. *190 pp.*
Farrell, C. My Mother Said. . . *A Study of the Way Young People Learned About Sex and Birth Control. 288 pp.*

Medicine, Illness and Society
General Editor W. M. Williams

Hall, David J. Social Relations & Innovation. *Changing the State of Play in Hospitals. 232 pp.*
Hall, David J. and **Stacey M.** (Eds) Beyond Separation. *234 pp.*
Robinson, David. The Process of Becoming Ill. *142 pp.*
Stacey, Margaret *et al.* Hospitals, Children and Their Families. *The Report of a Pilot Study. 202 pp.*
Stimson, G. V. and **Webb, B.** Going to See the Doctor. *The Consultation Process in General Practice. 155 pp.*

Monographs in Social Theory
General Editor Arthur Brittan

● **Barnes, B.** Scientific Knowledge and Sociological Theory. *192 pp.*
Bauman, Zygmunt. Culture as Praxis. *204 pp.*
● **Dixon, Keith.** Sociological Theory. *Pretence and Possibility. 142 pp.*
The Sociology of Belief. *Fallacy and Foundation. 144 pp.*
Goff, T. W. Marx and Mead. *Contributions to a Sociology of Knowledge. 176 pp.*
Meltzer, B. N., Petras, J. W. and **Reynolds, L. T.** Symbolic Interactionism. *Genesis, Varieties and Criticisms. 144 pp.*
● **Smith, Anthony D.** The Concept of Social Change. *A Critique of the Functionalist Theory of Social Change. 208 pp.*
● **Tudor, Andrew.** Beyond Empiricism. *Philosophy of Science in Sociology. 224 pp.*

Routledge Social Science Journals

The British Journal of Sociology. *Editor – Angus Stewart; Associate Editor – Leslie Sklair. Vol. 1, No. 1 – March 1950 and Quarterly. Roy. 8vo. All back issues available. An international journal publishing original papers in the field of sociology and related areas.*